PATCHWORK
& STITCHERY

CAROL PHILLIPSON

KRAUSE PUBLICATIONS
CINCINNATI, OHIO

14 13 12 11 10 5 4 3 2 1

DISTRIBUTED IN CANADA BY FRASER DIRECT
100 Armstrong Avenue
Georgetown, ON, Canada L7G 5S4
Tel: (905) 877-4411

DISTRIBUTED IN THE U.K. AND EUROPE BY
F+W MEDIA INTERNATIONAL
Brunel House, Newton Abbot, Devon, TQ12 4PU,
England
Tel: (+44) 1626 323200, Fax: (+44) 1626 323319
Email: postmaster@davidandcharles.co.uk

DISTRIBUTED IN AUSTRALIA BY CAPRICORN LINK
P.O. Box 704, S. Windsor NSW, 2756 Australia
Tel: (02) 4577-3555

www.fwmedia.com

Library of Congress Cataloging in Publication Data

Phillipson, Carol.

Patchwork & stitchery : 12 quilt projects with embroidered twists / Carol Phillipson. -- 1st ed.

p. cm.

Includes index.

ISBN 978-1-4402-0235-3 (pbk. : alk. paper)

1. Patchwork--Patterns. 2. Appliqué--Patterns. 3. Embroidery--Patterns. I. Title.

TT835.P5334 2010

746.46'041--dc22

2010017879

Edited by Layne Vanover
Production edited by Vanessa Lyman and Julie Hollyday
Designed by Rob Warnick
Production coordinated by Greg Nock
Photography by Ric Deliantoni

METRIC CONVERSION CHART		
To convert	**to**	**multiply by**
Inches	Centimeters	2.54
Centimeters	Inches	0.4
Feet	Centimeters	30.5
Centimeters	Feet	0.03
Yards	Meters	0.9
Meters	Yards	1.1

Acknowledgments

As always, I'd like to thank Alan for his continued help and support.

Also, I'd like to express my gratitude to Felicity for the beautiful appliqué in the *Flowers in Art* project.

My most sincere thanks to Judith Twambley (quiltedbyjude@yahoo.co.uk) for long-arm quilting the fronts exactly as I wished on fairly short notice. She quilted *Aegean Sea*, *Antique Rose*, *Roman Heads*, *Hedgerow Hexagons*, *Blue Floral Delight*, *Flowers in Art*, *Starry Flowers* and *Historical Blackwork Animals*.

Finally, thanks to Andrea Bishop and the technical support staff at Electric Quilt Company for solving an important problem.

About the Author

Carol Phillipson is a recognized cross-stitch and needlearts designer in the United Kingdom with many articles and exhibitions to her credit. She was a partner in Wrencraft Needlework kit producers. Carol is the author of several books on stitchery and patchwork, including *Designing Patchwork on Your Computer* (Krause Publications).

TABLE OF CONTENTS

For years I have enjoyed both embroidery and patchwork, but have treated them as separate entities. Only occasionally did I combine the two arts in one project such as a pillow or pincushion.

Some time ago I was sorting through my stash of fabric with the intention of stitching a Log Cabin quilt in reds and greens. I had been inspired by a wonderful array of poppies on the edge of a cornfield near my house. I love the shape and fragility of poppies and often incorporate them into projects.

A newly completed poppy pincushion was lying on my worktable next to the pile of red and green cottons, and it struck me that, together, they made an attractive combination. Why not stitch the pin-cushion design to replace some of the Log Cabin centers? What a pleasure it was to combine my all-time favorite quilt design with stitched poppies!

The seed for this book was well and truly sown. I started viewing other stitched pieces as potential additions to patchwork and was overwhelmed with possibilities. Combining the two gives an extra dimension and variety to the work.

This book shows just some of the possibilities. It is my hope that you will be inspired to use some of the patterns in it for your stitching, or to create some of your own.

Happy stitching,

Carol

Just as there are few quilters who haven't put an incomplete piece or two in the back closet, there are few stitchers who don't have at least one unfinished project lurking in both their cupboard and conscience. Why not dig these pieces out—quilts and stitchwork alike—and imagine what they might look like incorporated into one project? I'm confident you'll be pleased with the outcome!

Mixed quilts, those including both embroidery and patchwork, can arise from countless starting points. In this book, we'll focus specifically on five ways to bring these two crafts together into one artistic endeavor, with each approach enhancing the visual interest of your projects in unique ways.

Incorporating Stitching Into Traditional Designs

Often there are whole collections of cross-stitch designs in books or magazines which appeal to you, but where are you going to put eight or ten framed pictures? Imagine them instead as the centers of quilt blocks, serving as part of a lap quilt, a bed quilt, a lovely throw or even a wall hanging. For instance, the *Aegean Sea* (page 12) started as a framed bell-pull. However, when the designs were made up into a quilt, the result was much more striking.

Combining Stitchery With English Paper-Pieced Patchwork

Adding embroidered pieces such as diamonds, hexagons or octagons to patchwork created using the English paper-piecing technique not only highlights the extraordinary skill necessary to hand stitch pieces together, but also adds a subsequent layer of visual interest to a completed project. The stitched flowers in *Hedgerow Hexagon* (page 58), for example, act like detailed cameos in an overall floral pattern, both strengthening the countryside theme and nicely embellishing it.

Framing Stitchery With Patchwork

Personalized stitchery is a wonderful way to help someone celebrate a special occasion, whether it be a wedding, anniversary, birthday or christening. Not only is it a gift that can be treasured forever, but it also looks especially lovely when it is stretched, framed and hung on the wall. So why not take it a step further? Just imagine the visual interest you can add to a stitching project by framing it with patchwork and turning it into a quilted wall hanging! As *Edward Bear* (page 72) illustrates, patchwork can really enhance your stitching and give a gift that extra special touch.

Alternating Stitching With Pieced Blocks

Alternating stitching with pieced blocks is an excellent way to make each block of a quilt individually important. As such, this mixed quilt technique lends itself nicely to achieving a sampler effect, showcasing a number of unique blocks or panels. The *Flowers in Art* quilt (page 86) provides the perfect example of this: each letter stands out as it is framed by the alternating patchwork blocks.

Bordering Patchwork With Sashiko Stitching

The ancient Japanese art of *sashiko*—a method of stitching layers of fabric together using a simple running stitch—is a wonderful way to add zest to a quilting project. Incorporating decorative elements based on traditional Japanese designs, these simple, repetitive and interlocking patterns create interest even in the spaces between the stitching lines. As you'll see in *Sashiko Charm* (page 116), adding such decorative stitching to the borders of a quilt can really accentuate the overall design, in addition to unifying the theme.

Basic Supplies

- 6½" (16.51 cm) square ruler for trimming and sizing
- 6" × 24" (15.24 cm × 60.96 cm) plastic quilter's ruler
- Erasable fabric markers
- Iron and ironing board
- Pins and thimbles
- Quilting needles (Sharp 8-10)
- Rotary cutter
- Scissors for fabric and thread
- Scissors for cutting paper templates
- Self-healing mat (I recommend 23" × 17" [58 cm × 43 cm] for maximum benefit)

Whatever the trigger for combining embroidery and patchwork, there are two points to consider to ensure that they actually enhance each other.

Planning the Layout

It is easier to plan the stitching and patchwork for the entire quilt at once. In this way, the size of the stitched pieces can be adjusted to make the patchwork fit together well.

For appliqué or embroidery, you can simply photocopy the pattern or print it from the CD, altering the size to that required.

Using a counted thread design, the fabrics have a count or a tpi (thread per inch). For example, 14-count or 14 tpi means that there are 14 threads in every inch, so you work 14 stitches in every inch. If you wanted to use 28-count fabric, you could work the pattern over two threads to also get 14 stitches per inch.

Stitching a design on fabric with fewer threads per inch means fewer stitches per inch, so the design becomes larger. Similarly, working on fabric with a higher thread count means the design becomes smaller. To calculate the completed size of a piece of stitching, take the pattern size (number of stitches) and divide it by the number of tpi of the fabric. This will give the stitched size.

A slight alteration, such as working the stitching on 16-count instead of 14-count, can reduce the complexity of the patchwork calculations. It is meant to be fun, so make it easier for yourself. Working with a 12" × 12" (30.5 cm × 30.5 cm) patchwork block is far easier than working with one that measures 11⅝" (29.5 cm)!

Of course, if the stitching is already complete, then you must plan the patchwork around it. For example, if the stitching replaces a section of a repetitive pattern, such as in finished quilt blocks of *Poppy Log Cabin* on page 40, it becomes an integral part of the whole design.

Planning the Color Scheme

Color is an important consideration in linking the stitching with the patchwork. An obvious way to create a unified color scheme is to pick out colors from the stitching and use matching fabrics. The *Aegean Sea* quilt on page 12, demonstrates this idea well.

If possible, take your stitching threads with you when choosing fabric or vice versa, and lay the threads on top of the fabric. Stand back and squint to see if they harmonize.

READING COUNTED THREAD CHARTS

Each symbol on a chart represents one cross stitch in the corresponding color worked over one strand of Aida or two strands of evenweave. With embroidery floss, using two strands is the norm. The instructions will tell you when to use only one or more than two strands. Occasionally a symbol may indicate two colors, such as 46 / 24. This means that one strand of color 46 and one strand of color 24 should be used together to make up the two strands.

If stitches other than cross-stitch are to be used in a design, the instructions will make that clear.

1

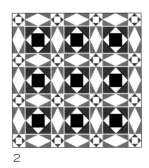

2

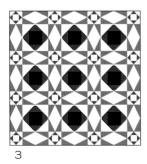

3

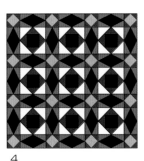

4

CONSIDERING COLOR

Before settling on a design, consider different color arrangements. Design 1 above, worked only in black and white, makes each individual stitching stand out. Designs 2 and 3 are identical except that the dark red and lighter triangles have been reversed, but design 3 looks much lighter. Design 4, with stronger coloring, is much richer.

Shopping by mail order and on the Internet has made a vast array of fabrics, threads and notions more readily available to all stitchers, even if there is no specialty shop nearby. However, it's important to note that because you will spend a great deal of time and energy stitching and making the quilts, it is worth buying good quality threads and fabrics. I know someone who spent a long time stitching a beautifully crisp embroidery in red and white with touches of green. She washed it carefully to remove a mark and ended up with pink undertones where the red had run, spoiling the whole stitching. She regretted buying threads cheaply from a market stall and learned a lesson the hard way: You receive the quality of goods for which you pay.

The fabrics used in this book fall roughly into three categories: Aida, evenweaves and fabric for surface embroidery. All should be of good quality so they will launder easily, making them suitable for inclusion in quilts.

Aida Fabric

This is a very evenly constructed blockweave fabric originally developed by Zweigart in the late nineteenth century. It comes in an array of colors with thread counts ranges from 6 tpi to 18 tpi. It also has clearly defined holes, making it easy to see and count. Cotton Aida is slightly cheaper than linen Aida.

Evenweave Fabric

There are many evenweave fabrics with thread counts ranging from 22 tpi to 45 tpi. As the name suggests, it is an evenly woven fabric, and as such, it produces a finer background for stitching than Aida; however, the holes are less clearly defined because of the smaller size. I invariably use an evenweave fabric, as I prefer its more refined appearance.

Stitching on evenweave is usually worked over two threads, so that a pattern worked on 28-count evenweave will be the same size when worked on 14-count Aida. This means that patterns for Aida and evenweave are interchangeable.

Evenweave also comes in many colors. It is worth bearing in mind that darker colors are not as easy to work on and light-colored threads can look muddy, although they can provide dramatic results.

Fabric for Surface Embroidery and Appliqué

This fabric should be more closely woven than fabric for counted thread work, as the needle needs to be able to enter any part of the fabric as the pattern dictates. Calico was used for the *Blue Floral Delight* quilt on page 78, cotton for the appliqué on the *Flowers in Art* quilt on page 86, and suiting fabric for the *Sashiko Charm* quilt on page 116. If the quilt will need to be laundered, check the washability of the fabric before using it.

Embroidery Threads

There is a mouth-watering array of threads available in stunning colors. Even after all the stitching I have done, new threads still excite me. However, most of the threads used here are stranded embroidery floss and Perlé cottons, both of which are readily available and will wash well without fading. Check on the durability of threads before using them.

Needles

Blunt-ended tapestry needles are best for counted-thread work, as they slide in the holes and don't split the threads. I find size 22 or 24 suitable for evenweave and 18 for wool in canvas. They have a large oval eye.

Embroidery needles have sharp points and an oval eye. Embroidery 5/10 are suitable for normal embroidery and Sharps 5/10 for fine embroidery.

Frames

Framing is a personal matter. I always use a rectangular or square frame, as I find it makes for neater work and helps the stitching keep its shape. There are many different types of frames, but I consistently use plastic clip-on frames, which are easy to put on and take off. Also, they don't damage the work, are very light to transport, and can be made up in different sizes.

Preparing the Fabric

To ensure successful laundering, choose 100 percent cotton fabric. Most cottons today are colorfast, but it is advisable to pre-wash fabrics prior to using them to make sure they will not fade or bleed. However, don't wash some fabrics and not others. It is a good idea to wash all or none of the fabrics; that way the shrinkage will be consistent when you do wash the quilt. Iron washed fabric while it is still damp to make it firm and crisp. All fabrics need to be ironed before cutting to ensure accuracy. Unless otherwise stated, the fabric requirements for the projects come from 42"-wide (106.6 cm-wide) fabric.

Rotary Cutting

Rotary cutting enables straight-edged shapes such as strips, squares and triangles to be cut quickly and accurately.

To straighten the edges of fabric, fold it in half with the selvedges together, then place it on the cutting mat, lining up the fold with the gridlines on the mat. Place the ruler at right angles to the fold, press down on the ruler to hold it firmly in place, and run the cutter along the side of the ruler.

Place the newly cut straight edge at the left side of the mat, then position the ruler over the cut edge until the edge of the fabric lines up with the size needed. Cut along the ruler. Remove the strip and repeat the procedure for the next measurement needed from this fabric. Always cut by the ruler measurements, not those on the mat. Use those for guidance only.

Piecing

Accuracy is the key to successful piecing. Cut patchwork pieces with a ¼" (6 mm) seam allowance.

To ensure accuracy when hand sewing, mark the ¼" (6 mm) seam line on the wrong side of the fabric and stitch on this line.

Sewing machines sometimes come with an integral ¼" (6 mm) seam guide or a ¼" (6 mm) foot, or you can buy one as an accessory. If you're unable to locate a ¼" (6 mm) seam guide or foot, fasten a piece of masking tape on the machine bed ¼" (6 mm) to the right side of the needle (not the presser foot). Use this as a guide for the fabric edge.

Test to make sure it is accurate, adjusting if necessary. Once it is in place, you can use it for all your seams.

Pin fabric pieces carefully, right sides together, and stitch from edge to edge on the seam line. Each seam needs to be pressed as soon as it is stitched. Use a dry iron and press gently rather than ironing firmly. Do the wrong side first, pressing the seam flat to set the stitches in place. Then press gently on the right side with both seams toward the darker fabric. Sometimes it may be necessary to press the seam open, but this will be specified in each project.

You will find the piecing templates in the book are also provided in the CD. Read the CD instructions for printing for the best accuracy.

Adding Sashing and Borders

Sashing is strips of fabric that frame the pieced squares. Borders are strips framing the completed quilt top. Instructions for adding these are given individually in the projects.

Preparing the Quilt Sandwich

A quilt sandwich consists of three layers: The pieced quilt top, a layer of batting and the backing. Note that the batting and backing need to be cut approximately 4" (10.2 cm) wider than the top to allow for uptake during quilting.

Press the pieced top and the backing before you begin. Next, spread out the backing wrong side up. Lay the batting on top of this and spread smooth. After you smooth the batting, lay the quilt top right side up, matching the centers, and pin and tack all three together. Start tacking in the center and work outward in rows approximately 4"–5" (10.2 cm–12.7 cm) apart until the quilt is covered with a grid.

Quilting and Binding

The three layers of the quilt sandwich need to be fastened together either by hand or machine quilting. The areas of stitching should be left unquilted, but quilting in the ditch around the stitched piece highlights it and sets it in place. Do this before quilting the remainder of the quilt.Once the quilt top has been quilted or secured, neaten the edges by trimming off excess batting and backing, and pin and stitch binding strips to all four sides.

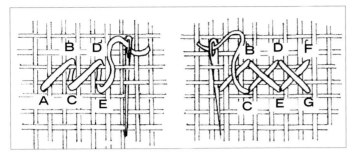

Cross-Stitch

Work over one thread on 14-count fabric and two on 28-count. To work a line, come up at (a), down at (b), up at (c), down at (d), up at (e), down at (f), and so on, then cross the stitches, up at (g), down at (d), up at (e), and so on.

To work single stitches, come up at (c), down at (d), up at (e), down at (b), up at (e), down at (f), and so on.

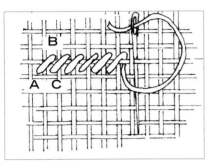

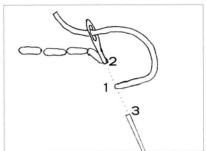

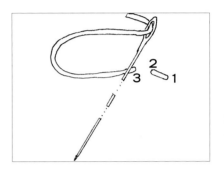

Half Cross-Stitch

Come up at (a), down at (b), up at (c), and so on.

Backstitch

Come up at (1), down at (2), up ahead at (3). Repeat, coming up ahead then going back.

Running Stitch

Come up at (1), down at (2), up at (3), and so on, keeping the stitches even.

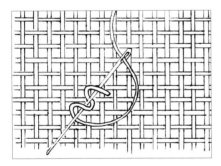

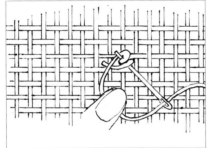

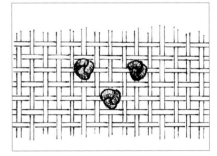

French Knot

Bring the needle through to the front of the work. Wrap the thread twice around the needle. Pull the loose end of the thread firmly, then, holding the thread firmly with your free hand, insert the needle through to the back of the work almost in the same hole. Pull gently until the knot lies on top of the work.

Stem Stitch

Come up at (1), down at (2) and up at (3) exactly half way between (1) and (2). Pull the thread through, keeping the thread below the needle. Repeat this, bringing the needle up in front and always keeping the thread below the needle and going back into the previous hole. A twisted rope effect will be formed.

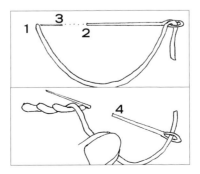

Reading the Cross-Stitch Charts

■ cross-stitch — backstitch

Note that unless otherwise stated in the instructions, a square on the cross-stitch chart usually indicates the use of a cross-stitch, while a straight line usually means you use a backstitch.

AEGEAN SEA

I've always been in awe of ancient Greek pottery. Knowing that such fragile clay vessels have managed to survive virtually intact for thousands of years despite heavy use is nothing short of amazing.

I find the decorative touches on these vessels particularly astonishing. Stories and customs are depicted beautifully in designs that are simple yet remarkable, and the wonderful bands of repetitive motifs found on the necks and bases are equally impressive. But what strikes me most is how the Greeks were able to successfully apply these embellishments without the use of paint. Rather, they simply treated the clay in a variety of clever ways to achieve different tones. The result was a limited yet attractive palette of colors, ranging from warm ochres to intense blacks. This palette inspired the color scheme for this quilt.

Some time ago I stitched a bellpull using a selection of six animal designs and borders taken from some of my favorite pottery vessels. However, I had a similar collection of drawings and photographs yet to be used, so I added another three designs for this lap quilt.

The *Storm at Sea* patchwork block was my first choice for this project, but I decided it would be too fussy and far too large, so I simplified the design. The outcome was *Aegean Sea*, my tribute to beautiful ancient pottery.

Materials

FOR THE STITCHERY

Nine 8½" (21.6 cm) squares 14-count Aida or 28-count evenweave fabric

6 skeins Anchor embroidery floss in 403 (black)

2 skeins Anchor embroidery floss in 897

1 skein Anchor embroidery floss in 307, 309, 310, 386, 890 and 901

FOR THE PATCHWORK

⅞ yd. (80 cm) black fabric

½ yd. (45.7 cm) tan fabric

¼ yd. (22.9 cm) gold fabric

¼ yd. (22.9 cm) red fabric

Batting and backing, 38½" × 38½" (97.8 cm × 98.7 cm)

Binding, ¼ yd. (22.9 cm) fabric for a 1½" × 136" (3.8 cm × 345.5 cm) strip

Inspiration for the *Aegean Sea* quilt

Aegean Sea
Finished size: 33½" x 33½" (85 cm x 85 cm)

Working the Embroidery

1. Following the charts and color keys, work each design in cross-stitch in the center of an 8½" (21.6 cm) square, using two strands of thread. If you prefer, you may work all of the designs on one larger piece and then cut them out. If you decide on the latter, allow 8½" (21.6 cm) of space for each design.

2. When all the designs are complete, spray lightly with starch and press on the back of the work, then trim to 6½" (16.5 cm), ensuring the design is in the center of the square. These squares are now ready to be incorporated into the patchwork.

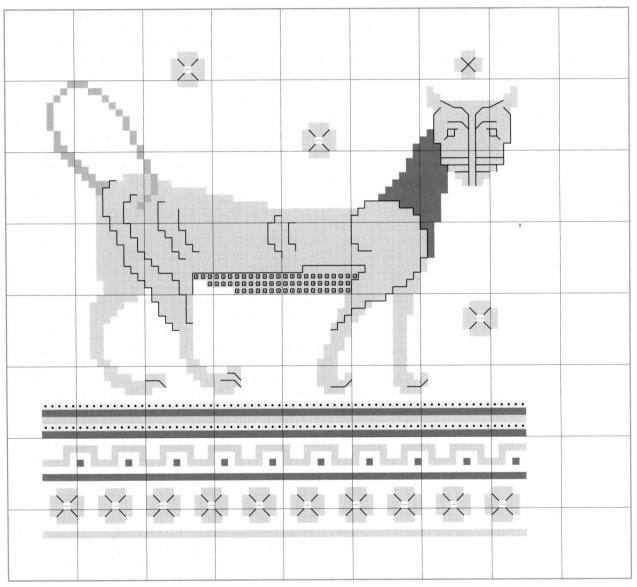

Cat

Anchor: 403 (black)

Anchor: 307 •   — Anchor: 386

Anchor: 309 ▣   ■ Anchor: 897

Anchor: 310   — Anchor: 386 × 2 strands

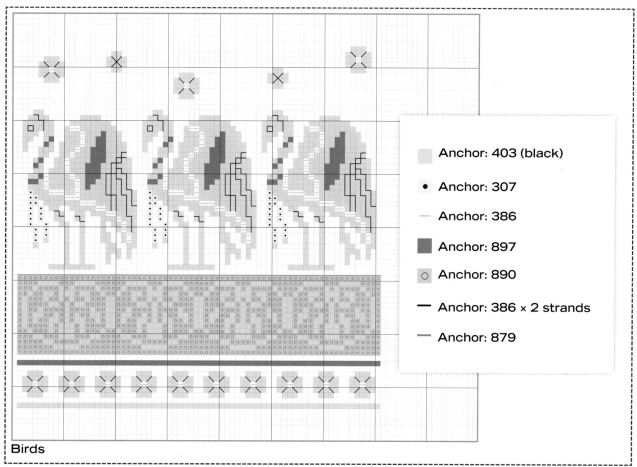

Anchor: 403 (black)

• Anchor: 307

— Anchor: 386

■ Anchor: 897

○ Anchor: 890

— Anchor: 386 × 2 strands

— Anchor: 879

Birds

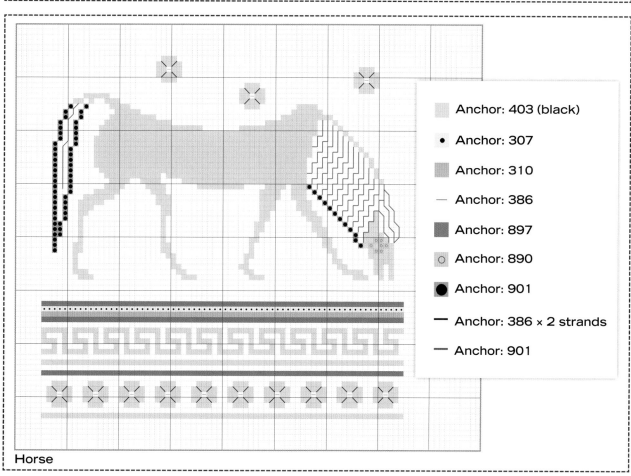

Anchor: 403 (black)

• Anchor: 307

Anchor: 310

— Anchor: 386

■ Anchor: 897

○ Anchor: 890

● Anchor: 901

— Anchor: 386 × 2 strands

— Anchor: 901

Horse

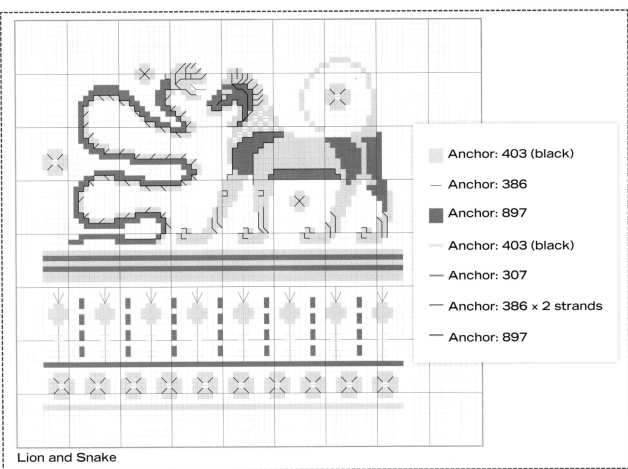

Anchor: 403 (black)

Anchor: 386

Anchor: 897

Anchor: 403 (black)

Anchor: 307

Anchor: 386 × 2 strands

Anchor: 897

Lion and Snake

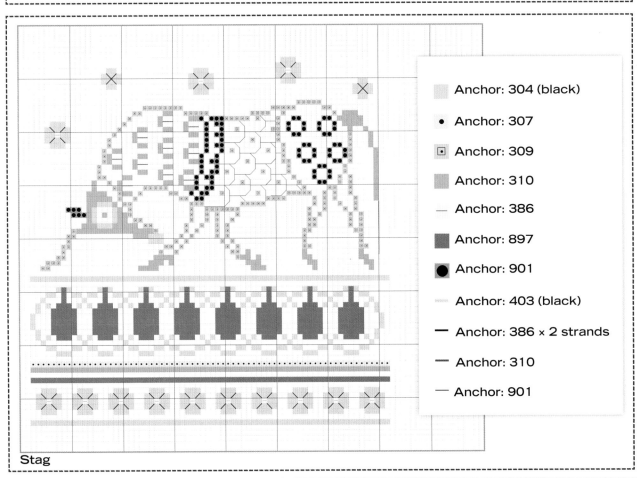

Anchor: 304 (black)

Anchor: 307

Anchor: 309

Anchor: 310

Anchor: 386

Anchor: 897

Anchor: 901

Anchor: 403 (black)

Anchor: 386 × 2 strands

Anchor: 310

Anchor: 901

Stag

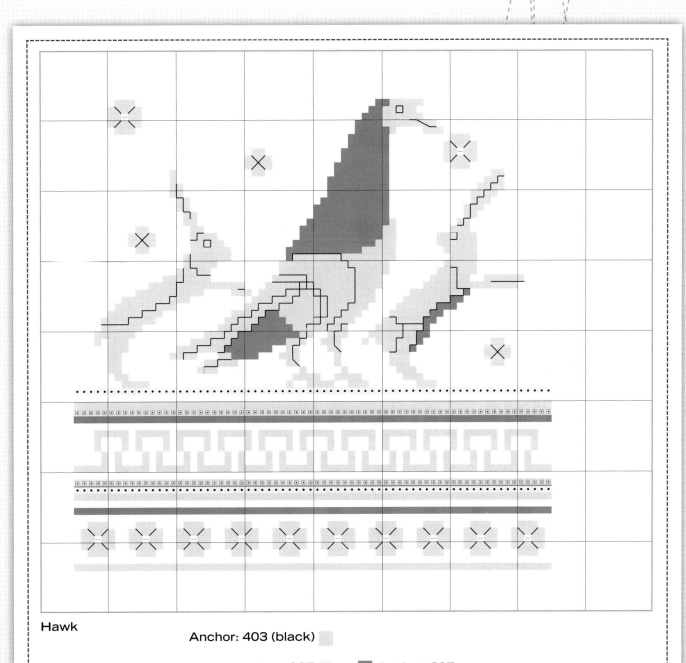

Hawk

Anchor: 403 (black)

Anchor: 307 •   ▓ Anchor: 897

Anchor: 309 ▣   — Anchor: 386 × 2 strands

Anchor: 386 —   ▬ Anchor: 897

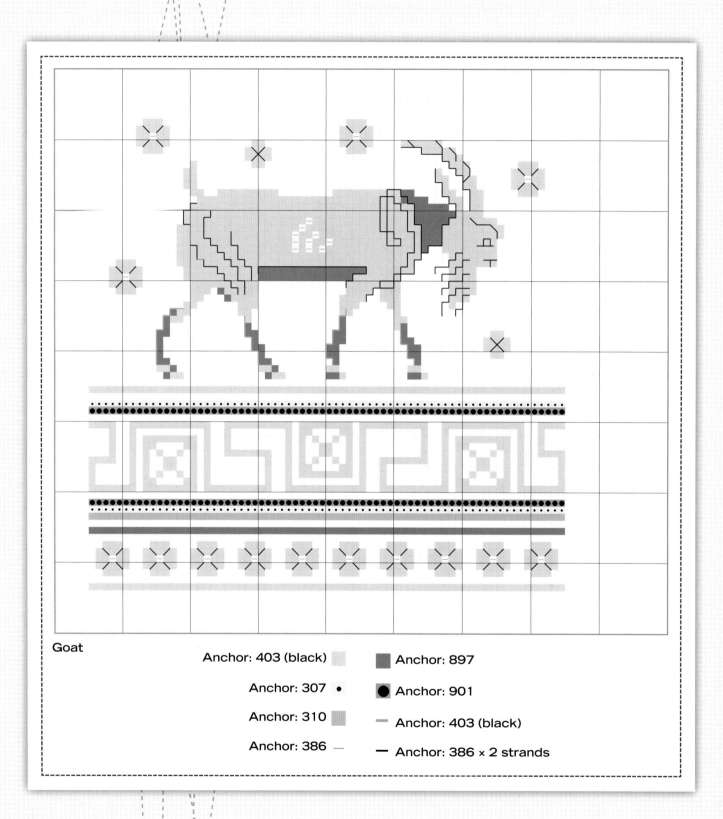

Goat

Anchor: 403 (black)		Anchor: 897
Anchor: 307 •		Anchor: 901
Anchor: 310		Anchor: 403 (black)
Anchor: 386 —		Anchor: 386 × 2 strands

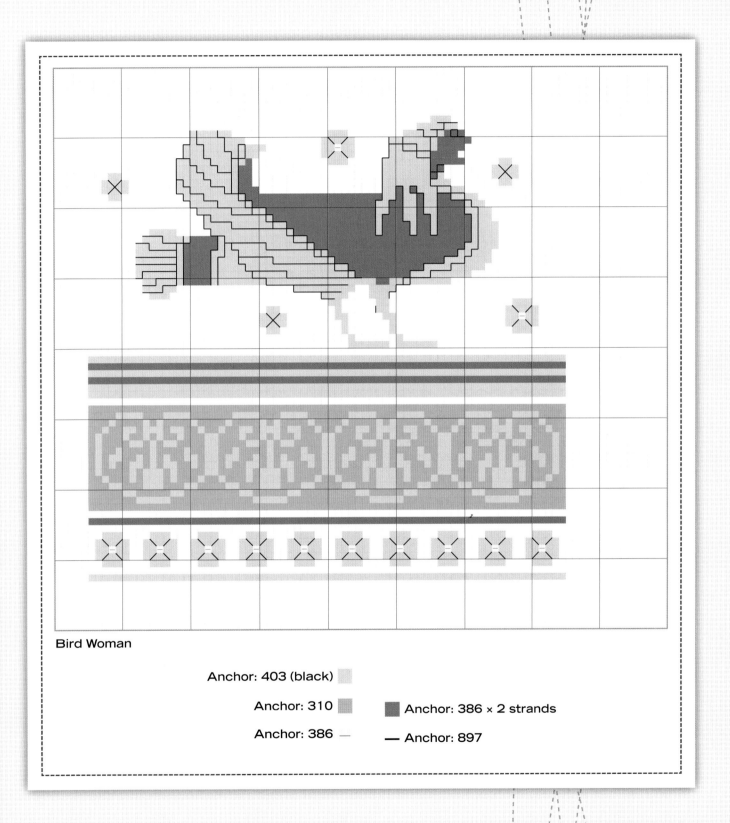

Bird Woman

Anchor: 403 (black)

Anchor: 310

Anchor: 386 × 2 strands

Anchor: 386 —

— Anchor: 897

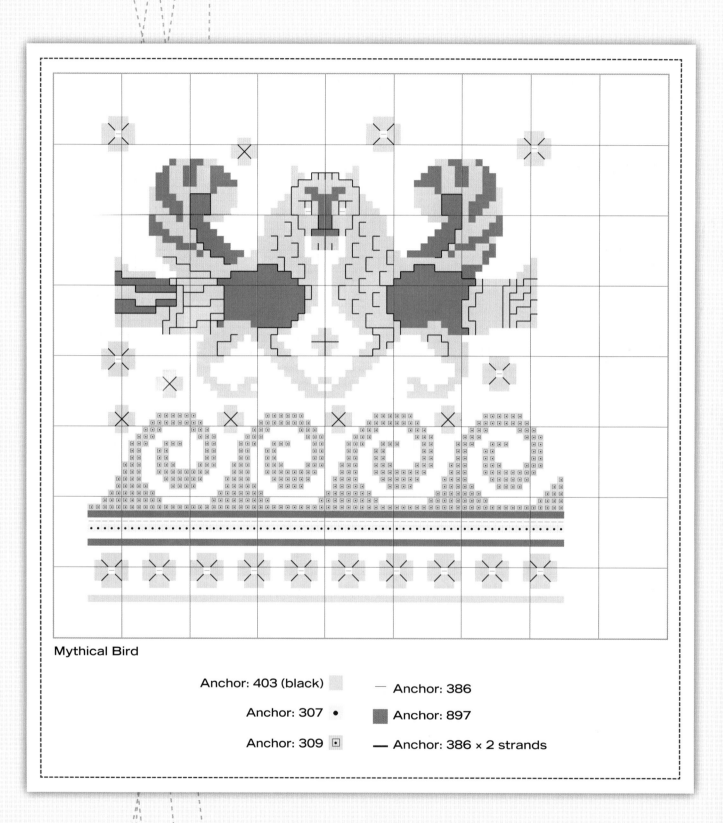

Mythical Bird

Anchor: 403 (black) — Anchor: 386

Anchor: 307 • Anchor: 897

Anchor: 309 ▣ — Anchor: 386 × 2 strands

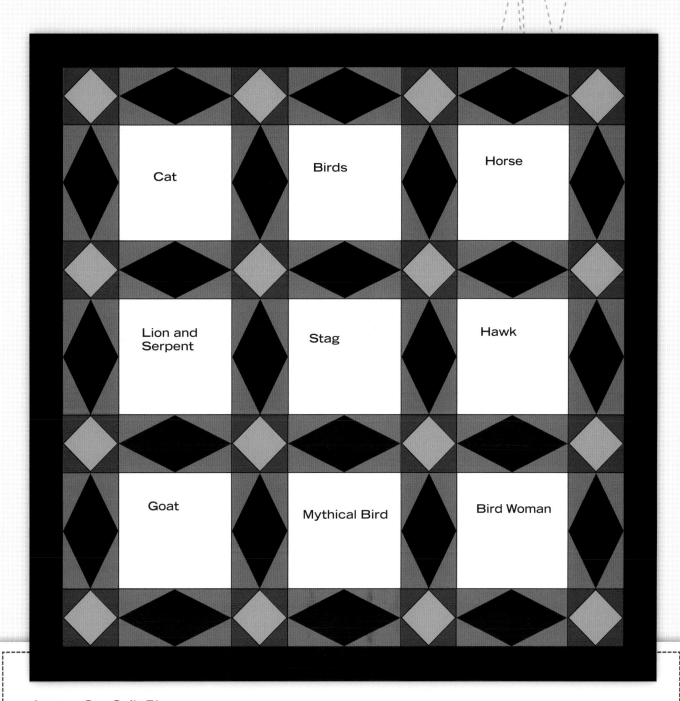

Aegean Sea Quilt Plan

This quilt is not made with complete blocks but rather the design is made up of two small units: a rectangle unit and a square unit. They are both made in the same way, using the templates provided.

Use ¼" (6 mm) seam allowances throughout. Each complete block measures 12" × 12" (30.5 cm × 30.5 cm).

Preparing the Patchwork

1. Cut four 2¼" × 36" (5.7 cm × 91.4 cm) strips from the width of the black fabric for the border.

2. Copy or print out the templates provided onto paper, then stick them onto a piece of card and carefully cut them out. If you wish, copy and cut them from template plastic.

3. For the diamond shapes, trace template C onto the wrong side of the remaining black fabric, cutting out a total of 24 diamonds.

   Trace templates A and B on the wrong side of the tan fabric and cut out 48 of each. Keep A and B in separate piles.

4. Position two A triangles along the opposite sides of a C diamond. With right sides together, pin and stitch the long sides. Press the seams away from the center.

   Pin and stitch two B triangles to the other two sides. Press the seams away from the center. You now have a 3½" × 6½" (8.9 cm × 16.5 cm) rectangle unit. Make 24 rectangle units total.

5. Using the second set of templates, cut 16 gold squares from template B and 64 red triangles from template A. Stitch four red corners on each gold square to make a 3½" (8.9 cm) red and gold square unit in the same way you made the rectangles. Make 16 units total.

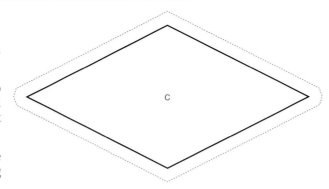

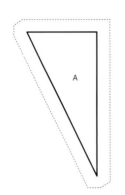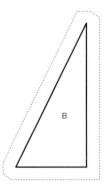

Templates A, B and C for the Rectangle Units
If copying, enlarge image by 200%

Pinning Two (A) Triangles to a (C) Diamond

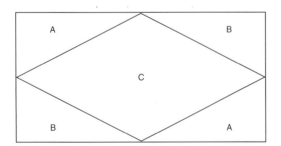

Completed Rectangle Unit
Not to size

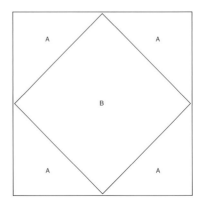

Completed Gold and Red Square Unit
Not to size

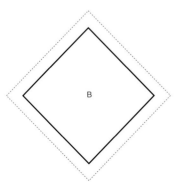

Templates A and B for Gold and Red Square Units
If copying, enlarge image by 200%

Making The Quilt Top

1. Following the quilt plan, lay out the top row as pictured in the diagram on this page. Pin and stitch the rectangles and square blocks together. Press the first seam to the right, the second to the left, the third to the right, and so on.

2. Lay out the second row, then pin and stitch the pieces together. Press all the seams away from the embroidery. The seams on row 1 should be pressed opposite to those on row 2, so when the rows are stitched together the seams abut each other.

3. Pin and stitch row 3, 5 and 7 following the same directions for pressing as for row 1.

   Pin and stitch rows 4 and 6, and then join the rows, following the same instructions as in step 2.

   Continue until all seven rows are stitched and the quilt top is complete.

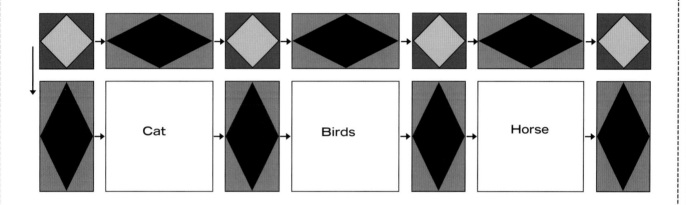

Adding the Borders and Finishing the Quilt

1. Trim the quilt top square, if necessary. Press well on the back.

2. With right sides together, pin a border strip to the left-hand side. The border will appear to be too long because it will become a mitered corner, so center the strip. Stitch the border to the quilt using a ¼" (6 mm) seam, starting and finishing your stitch lines ¼" (6 mm) from both ends. Refer to the instructions on pages 38–39.

3. Pin a border strip to the top edge of the quilt. Pin strip 1 out of the way. Stitch, starting and finishing ¼" (6 mm) from the ends. The stitching on strips 1 and 2 will share the corner hole.

4. Repeat with the other corners, then trim any excess to square up.

5. Make the quilt sandwich and quilt, then bind.

Mitered Corner (seam lies along the white line)

COUNTRYSIDE

Poppies are one of my favorite flowers. Whether it be an arrangement of glorious, showy oriental poppies or a plot of humble field poppies, I absolutely love the color and shape of their crinkly petals and dramatic centers.

This whimsical wall hanging provided me with the opportunity to stitch numerous poppy designs that originated from photographs I had taken. The little mouse was originally a much-loved paperweight design that seemed to complement the poppies perfectly, and the butterflies and rose hips not only matched the red, black and green coloring of the quilt, but also added further visual interest to the quaint countryside theme.

The stitched designs are small, so a simple alternate block suggestive of the poppy head shape was enough to complete the quilt effectively. I used a selection of charm blocks, so each flower is different. I also varied the black centers as well.

Any favorite small flower designs could be used in the same way, matching the alternate block color to corresponding flower colors.

Materials

FOR THE STITCHERY

Thirteen 4" (10.2 cm) squares of antique white 28-count evenweave or 14-count Aida

1 skein each of Anchor embroidery floss in 46, 47, 235, 266, 268, 335, 372, 403 and 943

Small amounts of Anchor embroidery floss in 1, 275 and 375

FOR THE PATCHWORK

¼ yd. (23 cm) light green; cut the following:

two 1" × 15½" (2.5 cm × 39.3 cm) borders

two 1" × 16½" (2.5 cm × 41.9 cm) borders

twenty-four 1½" (3.8 cm) squares

¼ yd. (23 cm) dark green; cut the following:

twenty-four 1½" (3.8 cm) squares

eight 1½" × 3½" (3.8 cm × 8.9 cm) rectangles

four 1½" × 2" (3.8 cm × 5.1 cm) rectangles

four 1½" × 1¾" (3.8 cm × 4.5 cm) rectangles

¼ yd. (23 cm) red; cut the following:

forty-eight 1½" (3.8 cm) squares

twelve 1½" × 3½" (3.8 cm × 8.9 cm) rectangles

⅛ yd. (11.5 cm) cream; cut ninety-six ½" (1.3 cm) squares

⅛ yd. (11.5 cm) brown; cut the following :

two 1" × 17" (2.5 cm × 43.2 cm) borders

two 1" × 18" (2.5 cm × 45.7 cm) borders

⅛ yd. (11.5 cm) black; cut the following:

two ¾" × 16½" (1.9 cm × 41.9 cm) borders

two ¾" × 17" (1.9 cm × 43.2 cm) borders

twelve 1½" (3.8 cm) squares

Batting and backing, 25½" × 25½" (64.8 cm × 64.8 cm)

Binding, ⅛ yds. (11.5 cm) for 1½" × 80" (3.8 cm × 203.2 cm)

12 medium-sized flatback buttons (optional)

Countryside
Finished size: 19½" × 19½" (49.5 cm × 49.5 cm)

Working the Embroidery

1. Work the designs in the center of each 4" (10.2 cm) square following the chart and key.

2. Spray lightly with starch and press the back of the embroidery, then trim to 3½" (8.9 cm) square. These squares are then ready to incorporate into the patchwork.

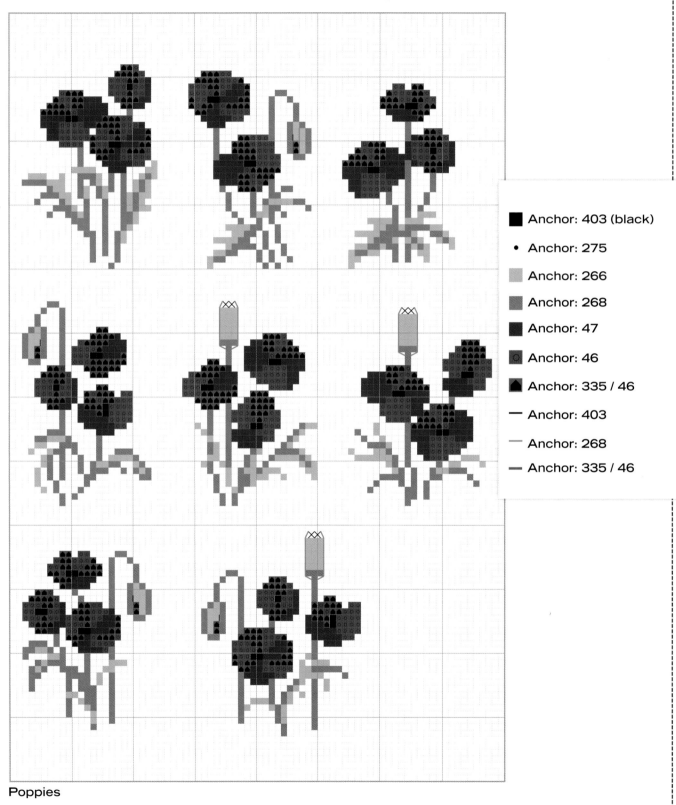

■	Anchor: 403 (black)
•	Anchor: 275
▨	Anchor: 266
▨	Anchor: 268
■	Anchor: 47
◉	Anchor: 46
⬟	Anchor: 335 / 46
—	Anchor: 403
—	Anchor: 268
—	Anchor: 335 / 46

Poppies

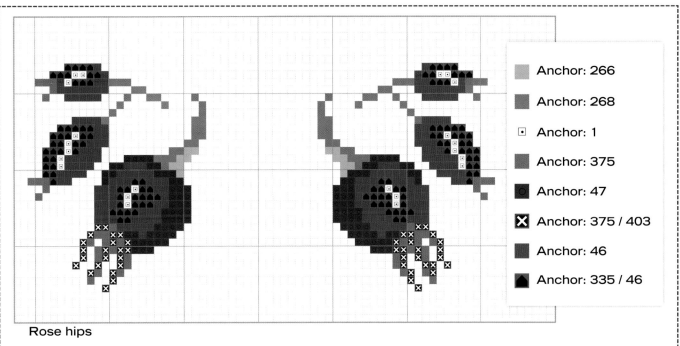

Rose hips

▦	Anchor: 266
▨	Anchor: 268
⊡	Anchor: 1
▨	Anchor: 375
⊙	Anchor: 47
☒	Anchor: 375 / 403
▪	Anchor: 46
⬢	Anchor: 335 / 46

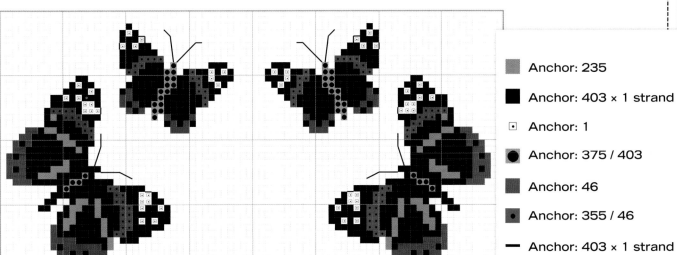

Butterflies

▨	Anchor: 235
■	Anchor: 403 × 1 strand
⊡	Anchor: 1
●	Anchor: 375 / 403
▪	Anchor: 46
•	Anchor: 355 / 46
—	Anchor: 403 × 1 strand

Mouse

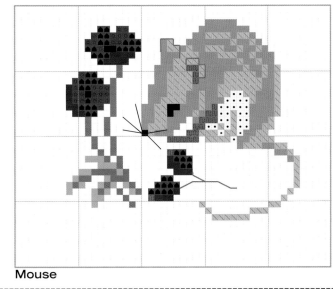

Anchor: 403	■	⋒ Anchor: 375	
Anchor: 275	•	▪ Anchor: 47	
Anchor: 266	▨	⊙ Anchor: 46	
Anchor: 268	▨	⬢ Anchor: 355 / 46	
Anchor: 943	▨	— Anchor: 403	
Anchor: 372	▨	— Anchor: 375	

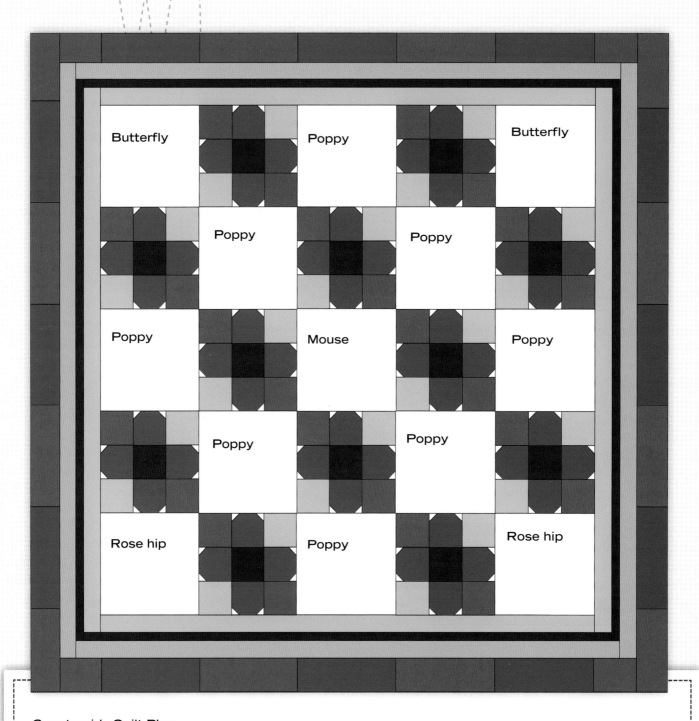

Countryside Quilt Plan

For extra decorative appeal, I added wooden buttons to the center of the four poppy heads surrounding the mouse (the four poppy blocks in the center) and small black beads to the side blocks. Refer to the finished quilt on page 24 for placement.

Use ¼" (6 mm) seam allowances throughout. Each finished block measures 3" × 3" (7.6 cm × 7.6 cm).

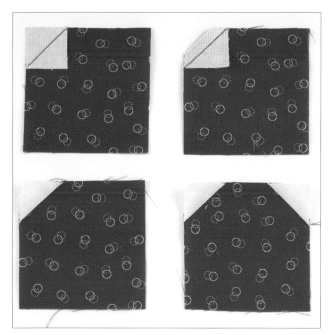

Preparing the Poppy Head Block

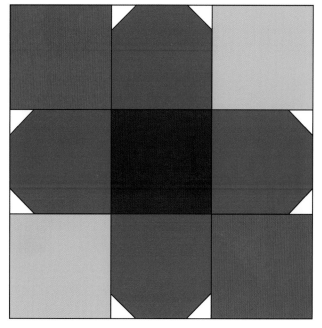

Block Plan

Preparing the Patchwork

1. First prepare the poppy head block. With right sides together, pin a ½" (1.3 cm) cream square to the corner of a 1½" red square. Draw a diagonal line across the cream square from edge to edge of the red square, then stitch along the line. Trim the seam to ¼" (6 mm) and press. Repeat this on an adjacent corner. The red square now has two adjacent cream corners.

   Follow the same process for the remaining 47 red units.

2. Following the block plan, pin and stitch the top row. Press the seams to the right. Do the same with row 2, but press the seams to the left. Press the seams of row 3 to the right.

3. Matching the seams carefully, pin and stitch the rows together to form the block.

4. To make the top pieced border, alternate three red and two dark green 1½" × 3½" (3.8 cm × 8.9 cm) rectangles, then add a 1½" × 1¾" (3.8 cm × 4.5 cm) dark green rectangle to each end. Repeat for the bottom border.

5. For the side border, alternate three red and two dark green 1½" × 3½" (3.8 cm × 8.9 cm) rectangles, then add a 1½" × 2" (3.8 cm × 5.1 cm) dark green rectangle at each end.

Making the Quilt Top

1. Following the quilt plan, lay out the entire quilt, then pin and stitch the poppy head blocks and embroideries together for the top row. Do the same for rows 2 through 5.

2. Matching the seams, pin and stitch the rows together. Press the seams open.

Adding the Borders and Finishing the Quilt

1. Stitch a 1" × 15½" (2.5 cm × 39.3 cm) light green border to the top and bottom of the quilt top. Then sew a 1" × 16½" (2.5 cm × 41.9 cm) light green border to each side.

2. Stitch a ¾" × 16½" (1.9 cm × 41.9 cm) black border to the top and bottom. Then sew a ¾" × 17" (1.9 cm × 43.2 cm) black border to each side.

3. Stitch a 1" × 17" (2.5 cm × 43.2 cm) brown border to the top and bottom. Then sew an 1" × 18" (2.5 cm × 45.7 cm) brown border to each side.

4. Sew the shorter pieced borders to the top and bottom of the quilt, and then sew the longer pieced borders to the sides.

5. Make the quilt sandwich and quilt. Add the binding.

6. Stitch the buttons to the black poppy head block centers.

The five small rose designs on this quilt were originally part of an anniversary cushion which was sold for charity, but I had always intended to stitch them again. This lovely lap quilt provided an ideal opportunity to do just that. The pattern for the cushion is included on the disk to enable you to stitch a matching cushion if you wish.

The quilt design is composed of alternate Pinwheel and Churn Dash blocks which are created using half-square triangle units. See pages 32-33 for details of stitching half-square triangle units.

The Original *Antique Rose* Anniversary Cushion

Materials

FOR THE STITCHERY

Five 6" (15.2 cm) 14-count Aida or 28-count Evenweave squares in Antique White

1 skein Anchor Embroidery floss in 260, 311, 860, 861, 894, 895 and 1027

Small amounts of 66, 49, 292, 293, 306, 340 and 386

Gold thread in an equivalent thickness of 2 strands of embroidery floss

FOR THE PATCHWORK

1½ yds. (1.4 m) dark pink; cut the following lengthwise:

two 2¼" × 47½" (5.7 cm × 120.7 cm) strips for the side borders

two 2¼" × 44½" (5.7 cm × 113 cm) strips for the top and bottom border

ten 5" (12.7 cm) squares

twenty 2½" × 4½" (6.4 cm x 11.4 cm) rectangles

four 2½" (6.4 cm) squares

1 yd. (.9 m) pink flower print; cut the following:

eight 2½" × 22" (6.4 cm × 55.9 cm) strips for the mitred border

twelve 2½" × 12½" (6.4 cm × 31.8 cm) sashing strips

four 3½" (9.8 cm) squares

¾ yd. (69 cm) cream flower print; cut the following crosswise:

eighteen 5" (12.7 cm) squares

eight 1" × 3½" (2.5 cm × 8.9 cm) rectangles

eight 1" × 4½" (2.5 cm × 11.4 cm) rectangles

¾ yd. (69 cm) green flower print; cut the following:

twenty 4½" (11.4 cm) squares

eight 5" (12.7 cm) squares

sixteen 2½" × 4½" (6.4 cm × 11.4 cm) rectangles

Batting and backing, 51½" × 51½" (131 cm × 131 cm)

Binding, ¼ yd. (22.9 cm)

Antique Rose
Finished size: 47½" x 47½" (120.7 cm x 120.7 cm)

Making Half-Square Triangle Units

Two squares can be stitched together, then cut to form two half-square triangle units. Each unit is then made up of two equal right triangles.

To allow for all the ¼" (6 mm) seam allowances, the squares need to be cut ⅞" (2.2 cm) larger than the finished size of the units. So, for a finished 4" (10.2 cm) unit, the original two squares need to be cut 4⅞" (12.4 cm). However, I prefer to cut them 1" (2.5 cm) larger and trim them. It uses very little extra fabric and gives a neater finish.

This method can be used for creating any design where half-square triangle units are needed, including Flying Geese.

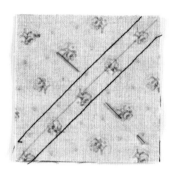

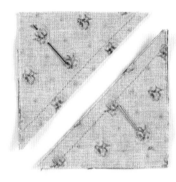

1. To make two 4" (10.2 cm) half-square triangle units, begin by cutting a 5" (12.7 cm) square from each of two fabrics and pin them right sides together. Press the fabric to help the pieces stick together during stitching.

2. Draw a pencil line lightly on the back of one of the squares across one diagonal. Machine sew ¼" (6 mm) on each side of the drawn line. If your machine doesn't have a ¼" (6 mm) foot, draw a ¼" (6 mm) line to guide the stitching. Use matching thread (contrasting thread was used in the sample to make the stitching obvious).

3. Using your ruler and rotary cutter or scissors, cut along the drawn line. You will now have two half-square triangle units.

4. Press each unit open from the front, pressing the seam allowance toward the darker fabric.

5. Trim to 4" (12.4 cm) using the diagonal mark on the ruler as a guide.

Flying Geese using half-square triangle units

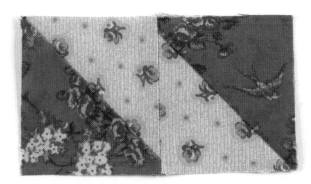

Diagonal stripe using half-square triangle units

Saw-tooth border using half-square triangle units

MAKING THE MOST OF YOUR FABRIC SCRAPS

A very effective scrap quilt can be made using half-square triangle units. Cut spare bits of fabric into 3" (7.6 cm) squares and keep them in a bag. When you have collected a good number, sort them into darks and lights. Join one dark and one light to make half-square triangle units. When you have a sufficient number of units for the size of quilt you wish to make, arrange them to form a pattern utilizing the dark and light tones. Stitch them together to make a quilt.

Working the Embroidery

1. Refer to the following pattern size:

Rose 1: 42 × 54 stitches; finished size of design 3" × 3.9" (7.6 cm x 9.8 cm)

Rose 2: 37 × 48 stitches; finished size of design 2.6" × 3.4" (6.7 cm × 8.7 cm)

Rose 3: 39 × 52 stitches; finished size of design 2.8" × 3.7" (7.1 cm × 9.4 cm)

Rose 4: 40 × 52 stitches; finished size of design 2.9" × 3.7" (7.3 cm × 9.4 cm)

Rose 5: 43 × 57 stitches; finished size of design 3.1" × 4" (7.8 cm × 10.3 cm)

2. Stitch all designs over each thread on 14-count fabric or over two threads on 28-count.

Work the design in the center of each square of fabric. You may find it easier to work all five designs on one larger piece of fabric, then cut out each individual design. Cut each design to 4½" (11.4 cm) square, making sure the design is centered in the fabric.

The design of Rose 5 is worked very close to the top and bottom edges. Adjust the length of the stem if necessary, because fabric's total thread count may vary slightly even though it is 14-count. Use 2 strands of cotton throughout.

Rose 1

✳	Anchor: Lamé Gold
•	Anchor: 66 / 49
▥	Anchor: 66
⊖	Anchor: 260
✦	Anchor: 292
▢	Anchor: 293
✳	Anchor: 306 / 293
�	Anchor: 311
▦	Anchor: 311 / 895
●	Anchor: 340
▼	Anchor: 340 / 861
∩	Anchor: 386 / 311
◥	Anchor: 386
▬	Anchor: 860
▨	Anchor: 861
✕	Anchor: 894
▽	Anchor: 895
▲	Anchor: 1027
⊚	Anchor: 1027 / 895

Key for All Rose Designs

Rose 2

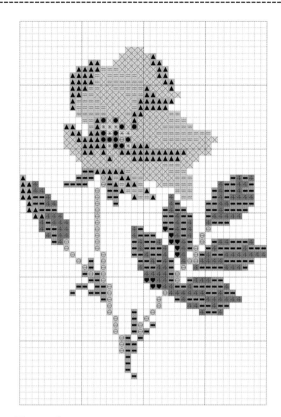

Rose 4

Rose 3

Rose 5

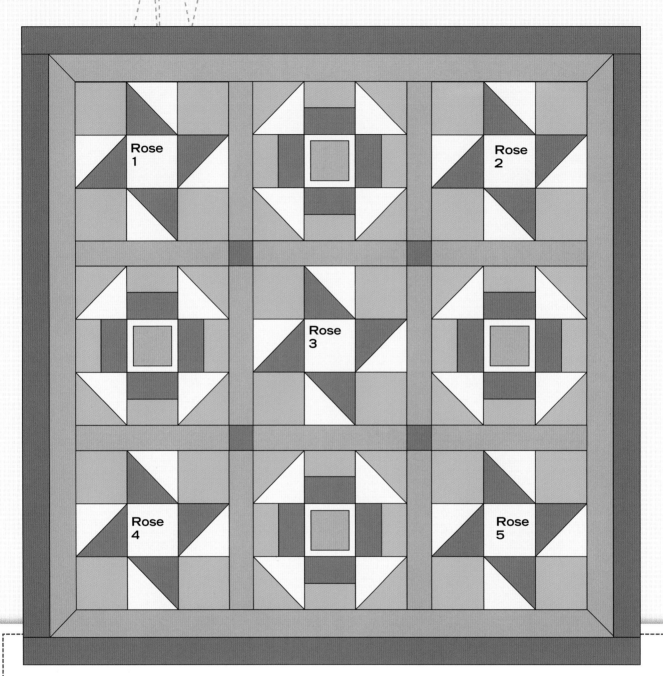

Antique Rose Quilt Plan

Use ¼" (6 mm) seam allowances throughout. Each finished block measures 12" × 12" (30.5 cm × 30.5 cm).

Making the Quilt Top

1. Using the method on pages 32-33, stitch sixteen cream flower and green flower half-square triangle units and twenty dark pink and cream flower half-square triangle units.

2. Stitch together sixteen pairs of dark pink and green flower rectangles to make sixteen 4½" (11.4 cm) square units.

3. Stitch a 1" × 3½" (2.5 cm × 8.9 cm) cream flower strip to opposite sides of each 3½" (8.9 cm) pink flower square. Then, stitch the 1" × 4½" (2.5 cm × 11.4 cm) cream flower strips to the tops and bottoms to form four 4½" (11.4 cm) center units.

4. Follow the plans to arrange the units to form five pinwheel blocks that have cross-stich flower centers, and four churn dash blocks.

5. Stitch the square units together in horizontal rows, then pin and stitch the rows together. You will now have nine 12½" (31.8 cm) blocks.

6. Stitch a pinwheel to a 2½" × 12½" (6.4 cm × 31.8 cm) pink flower sashing strip to a churn dash to a sashing strip to a pinwheel for the top row of the quilt. Stitch the third row of the quilt in the same way. For the middle row, stitch a churn dash to a 2½" (6.4 cm) pink flower sashing strip to a pinwheel to a 2½" (6.4 cm) pink flower sashing strip to a churndash.

7. Stitch a 2½" (6.4 cm) pink flower sashing strip to a 2½" (6.4 cm) dark pink square to a sashing strip to a dark pink square to a sashing strip for the horizontal sashing bands, then pin and stitch these to the bottom of rows 1 and 2. Then join the three rows, using the quilt plan for reference.

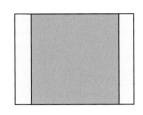

Churn Dash Centers

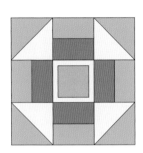
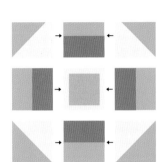

Churn Dash Plan

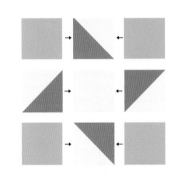

Pinwheel Plan

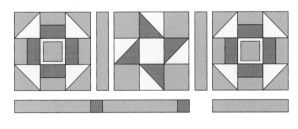

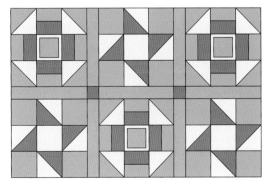

Adding Sashing

Adding the Borders and Finishing the Quilt

1. Stitch a 2½" × 4½" (6.4 cm × 11.4 cm) dark pink rectangle between two 2½" × 22" (6.4 cm × 55.9 cm) pink flower strips to form the border for one side. Repeat three more times.

2. Pin one border piece to the top of the quilt, right sides together, matching the dark pink and green flower rectangles so the border is centered. The border will be too long; this is to allow for the mitering. Starting and ending ¼" (6 mm) from the ends, (marked on Figure A by a dot) stitch the border in place. Press open.

3. In the same manner as step 2, pin and sew on border (b) to the left side of the quilt. With one border (a) pressed out and border two as it was stitched, not pressed back (b), draw a 45-degree line on the back of (b) to the edge. (Figure B)

4. Lay and pin borders (a) and (b), right sides together. The quilt corner will be folded in the center of the borders. (Figure B) Starting with the needle on the ¼" (6 mm) dot of the stitched seam line, stitch along the drawn line to the outer edge. (Figure C) Open out, and you should have a mitered corner. Check to make sure all is well, then trim the seam to ¼" (6 mm). Press the miter seam open. (Figure D) The dog-ears can be cut off when the quilt is finally squared off.

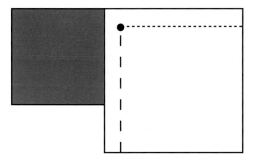

Figure A: Mark a pencil dot ¼" (6 mm) from the corner. Stitch borders in place starting and finishing at the dots

NOTE: In these samples, the yellow flowered fabric represents the quilt corner and the red represents the border

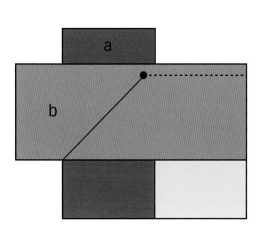

Figure B: With one border seam pressed back in place (a) and border two as it was stitched, not pressed back (b), draw a 45-degree line on the back of (b) to the edge.

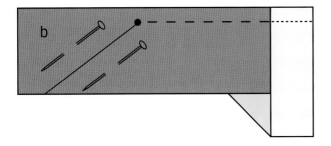

Figure C: Lay and pin borders (a) and (b) right sides together with the quilt corner folded in the center. Stitch the drawn line from dot to the outer edge. Trim seam to ¼" (6 mm).

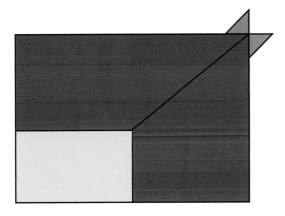

Figure D: Open out and press. Front view of mitered corner

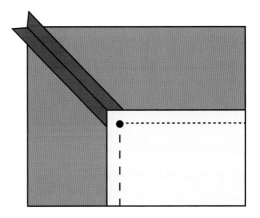

Figure D: Back view of mitered corner

5. Stitch the miters on the other three corners in the same way and trim the quilt to 44½" (113 cm) square.

6. Pin and stitch a dark pink 2¼" × 44½" (5.7 cm × 113 cm) border strip to the top and bottom of the quilt and press. Stitch a 2¼" × 47½" (5.7 cm × 120.7 cm) border strip to the right and left sides. Press open.

7. Put the quilt sandwich together and trim, and then quilt as you wish.

8. Add a 1½" (3.8 cm) binding strip, fold it to the back, then slipstitch in place, turning in a ¼" (6 mm) hem.

POPPY LOG CABIN

The Log Cabin design has been popular since the mid-nineteenth century, when quilts were raffled by the Union army to raise money to fight the Civil War. It represents the early American log cabin home, with "logs"—strips of fabric—placed in a specific order around a central square to make a block. Traditionally, this square was red, representing the heart of the home: the fire. Two sides of the block were light in color to indicate the fire's light, while the other two were dark in color, to suggest the shadows cast.

You can make numerous arrangements using the basic block, each forming a different pattern. Some popular examples include Sunshine and Shadow, Pinwheels and Barn Raising.

You can also vary the design by replacing part of a Log Cabin block with stitchery, as long as there is at least one log strip at the edge to join it to the next block. Complete Log Cabin blocks could be replaced by stitchery as well, but this may split the overall Log Cabin design of the quilt.

As you can see, the arrangement used for this project is a variation of Barn Raising, with the center squares in the four corner blocks replaced by stitched poppies.

Materials

FOR THE STITCHERY

1 skein Anchor embroidery floss in 46, 47, 266, 268, 335, 403

Four 6" (15.2 cm) of 14 or 22-count evenweave or Aida for each stitched poppy

FOR THE PATCHWORK

1½ yds. (1.4 m) assorted light/medium greens

1½ yds. (1.4 m) assorted dark greens for outer strips of logs and center sashing

1½ yds. (1.4 m) assorted light/medium creams

1½ yds. (1.4 m) assorted dark reds

½ yd. (0.5 m) assorted light reds

3 yds. (2.7 m) assorted medium reds

Eight 1½" (3.8 cm) squares of contrasting fabric for the red/green block centers

Eight 1½" (3.8 cm) squares of contrasting fabric for the red/cream block centers

1 fat quarter of black for the poppy centers and border

Backing and batting, 50" × 71" (127 cm × 180.3 cm)

4 medium button and 16 small buttons for block centers (optional)

Alternative binding, ½ yd. (.46 m) (optional)

Variations on the Log Cabin Design

Three popular arrangements, pictured left to right: Sunshine and Shadow, Pinwheels and Barn Raising.

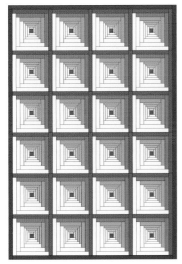 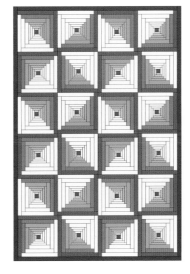 

Poppy Log Cabin
Finished size: 46" × 67" (116.8 cm × 170.5 cm)

Working the Embroidery

1. Work one stitch over every thread. If you work the poppies on 22-count evenweave or Aida, use one strand. If you use 14-count fabric, use two strands. No matter which type of fabric you use, the design will be 58 × 60 stitches, but the size of the finished unit will depend on the fabric's thread count.

2. Iron your finished stitchery on the wrong side. You may find it helpful to use spray starch, which will temporarily give the fabric more body and make it easier to handle. Cutting instructions for the stitchery is in the following pages.

Poppy Chart and Key

Finished Stitchery Unit

■	Anchor: 403
⊙	Anchor: 266
⊠	Anchor: 268
✚	Anchor: 47
▨	Anchor: 46
•	Anchor: 335

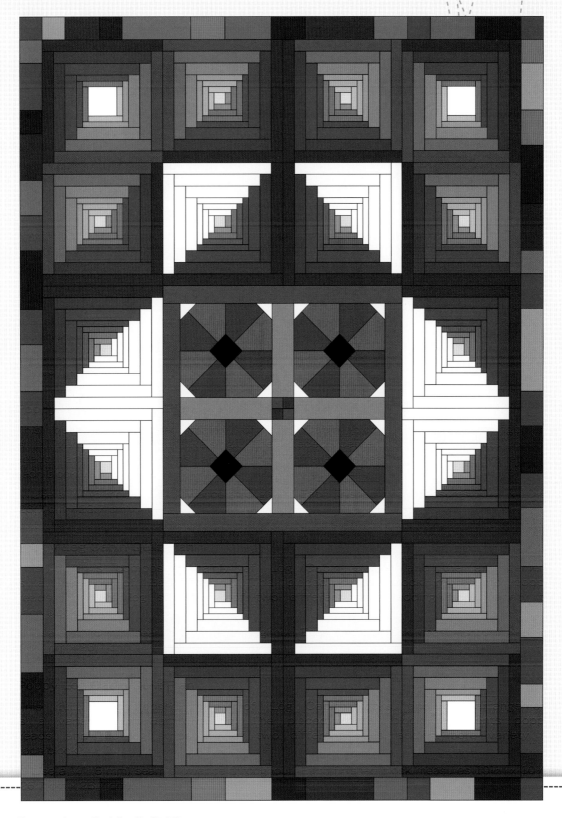

Poppy Log Cabin Quilt Plan

This quilt is composed mainly of Log Cabin blocks, and the arrangement is a variation of Barn Raising. The pieced center block represents poppy heads, and the log strips are of two different sizes, adding more variety to each block.

Use a ¼" (6 mm) seam allowance throughout. Each finished block measures 10½" × 10½" (26.7 cm × 26.7 cm).

Making the Poppy Head Blocks

1. Choose eight contrasting reds for the poppy heads, cutting two 5" (12.7 cm) squares from each.

2. Place two squares right sides together, then draw a diagonal line across the back of one and pin them together. Stitch them together, ¼" (6 mm) from each side of the drawn line, then cut along the line to make two half-square triangle units (see page 32). Press the seams open and trim to form two 4½" (11.4 cm) squares, ensuring the seam is on the diagonal.

3. Repeat with the other squares. You will now have sixteen 4½" (11.4 cm) half-square triangle units.

4. With the cream of your choice, cut sixteen 2½" (6.3 cm) squares. Also cut sixteen 1½" (3.8 cm) black squares. On the back of each square, draw a light pencil line across one diagonal.

5. With right sides facing, line up and pin a cream square on one corner of one of the 4½" (11.4 cm) red half-square triangle units, then stitch along the drawn line. Trim the seam to ¼" (6 mm). Line up and stitch a black square to the opposite corner. Trim to ¼" (3 mm). Repeat this with each half-square triangle, then press all the seams towards the center. (Figure A)

6. Arrange the sixteen completed units into four poppy head blocks, with the black corners at the center. Stitch together to make the four 8½" (21.6 cm) poppy head blocks. (Figure B)

7. From dark green, cut four 8½" × 2½" (21.6 cm × 6.3 cm) pieces. Pin and stitch one piece to one side of a poppy head block. Stitch a poppy head block on the other side. Repeat this with the other two poppy head blocks. (Figure C)

8. Cut two 1½" (3.8 cm) squares from two different reds, joining them first in two pairs and then together, to make a four-patch for the center. Stitch one of the remaining green strips to one side of the foursquare. Stitch the remaining strip to the opposite side. (Figure D)

9. Connect your two poppy head panels with the second strip. (Figure E)

10. From dark green, cut two 2" × 18½" (5 cm × 47 cm) pieces and two 2" × 21½" (5 cm × 54.6 cm) pieces.

11. Pin and stitch the short pieces to opposite sides of the center block and press. (Figure F)

12. Pin and stitch the long pieces to the remaining sides and press. The poppy head center is now complete.

Assembling the Poppy Head Block

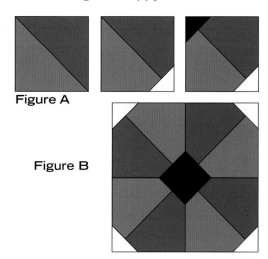

Figure A

Figure B

Assembling the Poppy Head Center

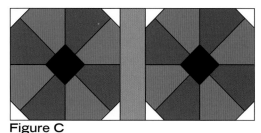

Figure C

Figure D

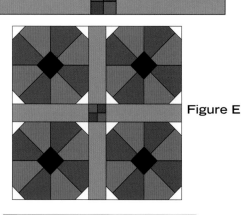

Figure E

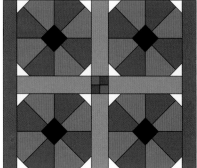

Figure F

Making the Red and Green Log Cabin Blocks

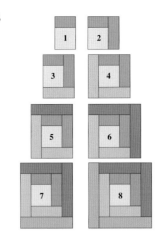

1. Cut a 1" × 1½" (2.5 cm × 3.8 cm) strip from the palest red fabric. With right sides together, stitch this to one edge of a 1½" (3.8 cm) color square. Press away from the center.

2. Cut a 1" × 2" (2.5 cm × 5 cm) length from your palest red, and following the sequencing plan, pin, stitch and press away from the center.

3. From the palest green 1 strip, cut a 1" × 2" (2.5 cm × 5 cm) length and stitch to the block. Continue in the same way, following the plan until the block is complete. The sizes to cut for each piece are:

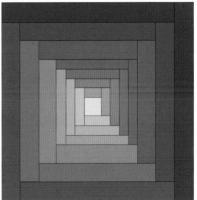

1: 1" × 1½" (2.5 cm × 3.8 cm)

2, 3: 1" × 2" (2.5 cm × 5 cm)

4, 5: 1" × 2½" (2.5 cm × 6.3 cm)

6, 7: 1" × 3" (2.5 cm × 7.5 cm)

8, 9: 1" × 3½" (2.5 cm × 8.8 cm)

10, 11: 1" × 4" (2.5 cm × 10.1 cm)

12, 13: 1" × 4½" (2.5 cm × 11.4 cm)

14: 1" × 5" (2.5 cm × 12.7 cm)

15: 1½" × 5" (3.8 cm × 12.7 cm)

16, 17: 1½" × 6" (3.8 cm × 15.2 cm)

18, 19: 1½" × 7" (3.8 cm × 17.8 cm)

20, 21: 1½" × 8" (3.8 cm × 20.3 cm)

22, 23: 1½" × 9" (3.8 cm × 22.8 cm)

24, 25: 10½" × 10½" (26.7 cm × 26.7 cm)

26: 1½" × 11" (3.8 cm × 28 cm)

Note: When stitching these blocks together, be especially careful with your seam allowances; even being slightly off can drastically effect the finished size of the blocks.

Assembling a Log Cabin Block

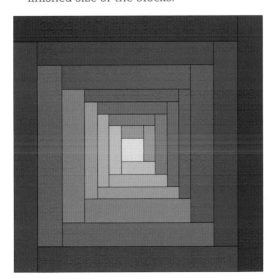

Red and Green Log Cabin Block

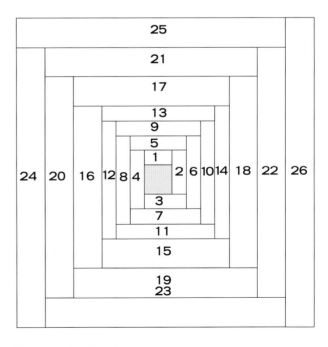

Sequencing Plan

Making the Red and Cream Log Cabin Blocks

1. Make eight red and cream Log Cabin blocks following the steps used to create the red and green blocks (page 45). Substitute the cream for green. The finished block should be 10½" × 10½" (26.7 cm × 26.7 cm)

Red and Cream Log Cabin Block

Making the Stitchery Blocks

1. Measure your completed embroidery, adjusting the size so it fits into one of the sizes of Log Cabin squares. Read on before cutting.

2. If your stitching is 2½" (6.3 cm), allowing for a small border, it will replace logs 1 through 6. If it is 4½" (11.4 cm), it will replace logs 1 through 12, so you will start adding at number 13.

3. You will need to add the ¼" (6 mm) seam allowance before cutting, which means adding ½" (1.3 cm) to the stitched size. So, for 2½" (6.3 cm) cut 3" (7.5 cm), and for 4½" (11.4 cm) cut 5" (12.7 cm). Remember to make sure the design is in the center.

4. Assemble the stitchery blocks as for the Log Cabin blocks (page 45), replacing the center pieces with your stitchery units.

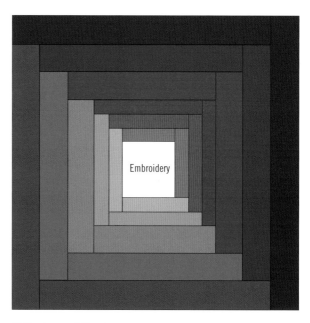

Stitchery Block

Making the Quilt Top

1. Trim the completed blocks to 11" (27.9 cm) if necessary. Lay out the blocks before stitching, following the plan.

2. Make up the central poppy head section as shown in the figure A. First, join the two cream and red blocks, then stitch them to the central panel.

3. Join the blocks in rows, then stitch the rows together matching seam lines carefully.

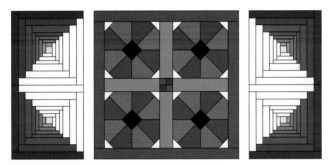

Figure A: Assembling the Poppy Head Section

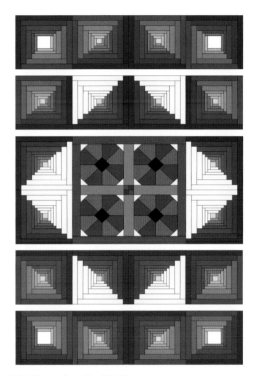

Making the Quilt Top

Adding the Border

1. The poppy quilt has a 2" (5 cm) border that turns over to the back to create a wide binding. This gives a lovely edge to the back of the quilt. This is made from several 4½" (11.4 cm) wide pieces cut at random lengths from fabric pieces left over from the quilt. I cut the four corners from the same fabric, so they needed to be 2½" × 4½" (5.7 cm × 11.4 cm).

2. Stitch enough pieces together to make two 4½" × 42½" (11.4 cm × 106.7 cm) strips. Stitch these to the top and bottom of quilt.

3. Stitch enough pieces together to make two 63½" (161.3 cm) strips and add a corner to each end, yielding a total length of 67½" (171.3 cm). Stitch these strips to the sides of the quilt.

4. Make a quilt sandwich with the quilt top, batting and backing. Quilt as desired. Being careful not to the border fabric and backing, trim the batting to 2" (5 cm) from the edge of the quilt top. Turn over the border as a binding. On the back, turn the border under a ¼" (6 mm) hem and slip stitch.

5. **For the alternative binding:** You could make a 2" (5 cm) border, then bind the edges as usual. In this case, make two 2½" × 42½" (6.3 cm × 108 cm) strips for the top and bottom, then add two 2½" × 67½" (6.3 cm × 171.3 cm) strips for the sides.

6. If you choose, you can add small black buttons in the center of each Log Cabin block and larger black buttons in the center of the poppy heads.

ROMAN HEADS

This quilt is based on the pattern of a tiled floor in the chancel of Santa Maria dei Miracoli in Venice. The square diamond pattern of this floor was perfect for accommodating the embroideries, which were inspired by Roman floor mosaics found in the British Museum.

Initially, I sorted out the fabrics and made up a pieced quilt top. It was only as I completed the top that I realized it would be much easier and more accurate to make the same design using foundation piecing, a useful method outlined on page 50. So, I picked out the stitches and remade the top!

I used 19-count evenweave fabric, working over every thread. Because the design is foundation-pieced, the plans can be enlarged on a photocopier if you wish to use fabric with a different count. However, bear in mind that if you change the size, you will need to adjust the amounts of the materials, the lengths of borders, etc.

Materials

FOR THE STITCHERY

Two 7½" (19 cm) 19-count evenweave squares

1 skein of Anchor Embroidery floss in 142, 275, 338, 378, 390, 880, 869, 871, 874 and 886

Small amounts of Anchor Embroidery floss in 231, 276, 341, 387, 870, 1082 and 4146

FOR THE PATCHWORK

½ yd. (45.7 cm) assorted grays for the foundation piecing

½ yd. (45.7 cm) assorted creams for the foundation piecing

¼ yd. (23 cm) dark gray for the centers of the foundation piecing

¼ yd. (23 cm) dark sand for the centers of the foundation piecing

½ yd. (45.7 cm) dark and light terracotta for the squares

⅛ yd. (11.5 cm) light gray for the centers of the squares

⅛ yd. (11.5 cm) cream for the centers of the squares

½ yd. (45.7 cm) gray for the borders

¼ yd. (23 cm) cream for the borders

Backing and batting, 35" × 46" (88.9 cm × 116.8 cm)

Binding, ¼ yd. (23 cm) for 1½" × 142" (3.8 cm × 360.7 cm)

Roman Heads
Finished size: 29" × 41" (73.6 cm × 104.1 cm)

49

Foundation Piecing

Foundation piecing is a method for ensuring absolute accuracy when piecing small designs that would be difficult to reproduce by traditional stitching. One of the greatest advantages of this method is that identical blocks can be produced many times over with ease.

Pattern lines and numbers are drawn onto a foundation and the stitching follows these drawn lines according to a numerical sequence. Best of all, fabric doesn't have to be cut accurately because it is trimmed after each seam.

With smaller designs, I prefer to tear away the foundation, so I use thin paper, such as tracing paper or printer paper. However, a fine fabric foundation, such as muslin, could be left in larger designs to give more stability.

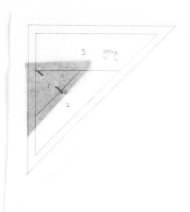

1. Transfer the pattern unit and numbers to the foundation by placing the foundation over the pattern and tracing it using a ruler and sharp pencil. Cut out the unit, leaving at least 1" (1.5 cm) border. Repeat this for the number of stitched units needed.

Cut a piece of fabric for section 1 that is at least ½" (1.3 cm) bigger all the way around. Pin this to the back of the foundation, then trim the edge to ¼" (6 mm) beyond the line that separates sections 1 and 2.

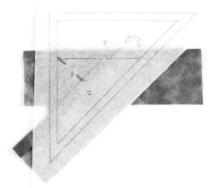

2. Cut a piece of fabric for section 2, again leaving a border. With right sides together, looking through the foundation to place it, pin this over section 1, leaving at least ¼" (6 mm) over the line between sections 1 and 2. Fold the back of the foundation and trim the seam line to ¼" (6 mm). Fold piece 2 over the seam and press with a dry iron.

3. Repeat for remaining sections.

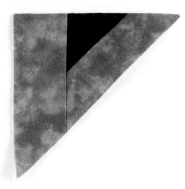

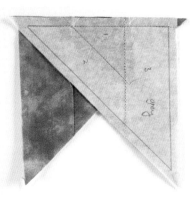

4. Trim the foundation fabrics as needed to match the seam allowances on the pattern.

5. Keep the paper foundations in the blocks until all the patchwork is complete; this will prevent any stretching. The papers can then be removed, the stitching acting as perforations.

Working the Embroidery

1. Following the charts and color key, work one head in cross-stitch in the center of each piece of fabric.

2. When complete, lightly spray the wrong side with starch and press. Trim to 4½" (11.4 cm), keeping the design in the center. If the evenweave is likely to fray, overcast the edges. The designs are now ready to be used as part of the pieced quilt.

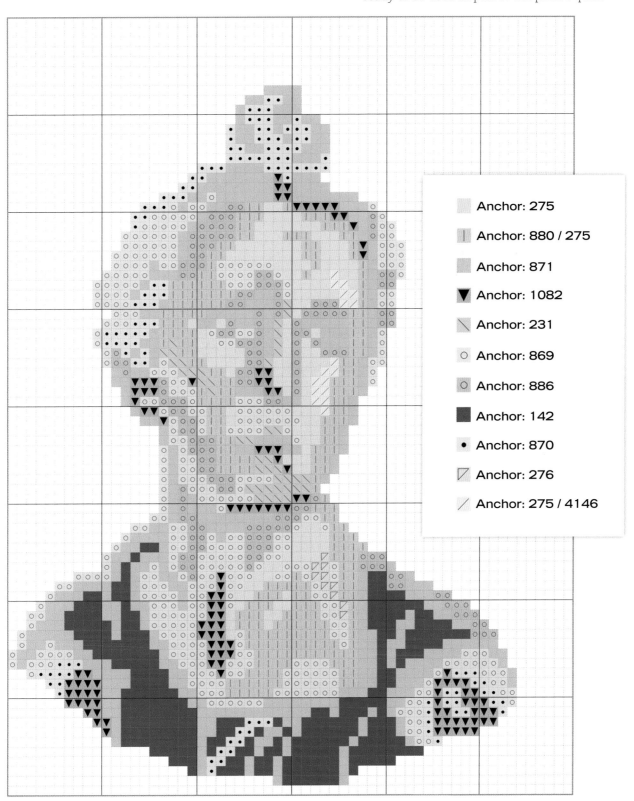

	Anchor: 275
	Anchor: 880 / 275
	Anchor: 871
▼	Anchor: 1082
╲	Anchor: 231
○	Anchor: 869
◎	Anchor: 886
■	Anchor: 142
•	Anchor: 870
▱	Anchor: 276
╱	Anchor: 275 / 4146

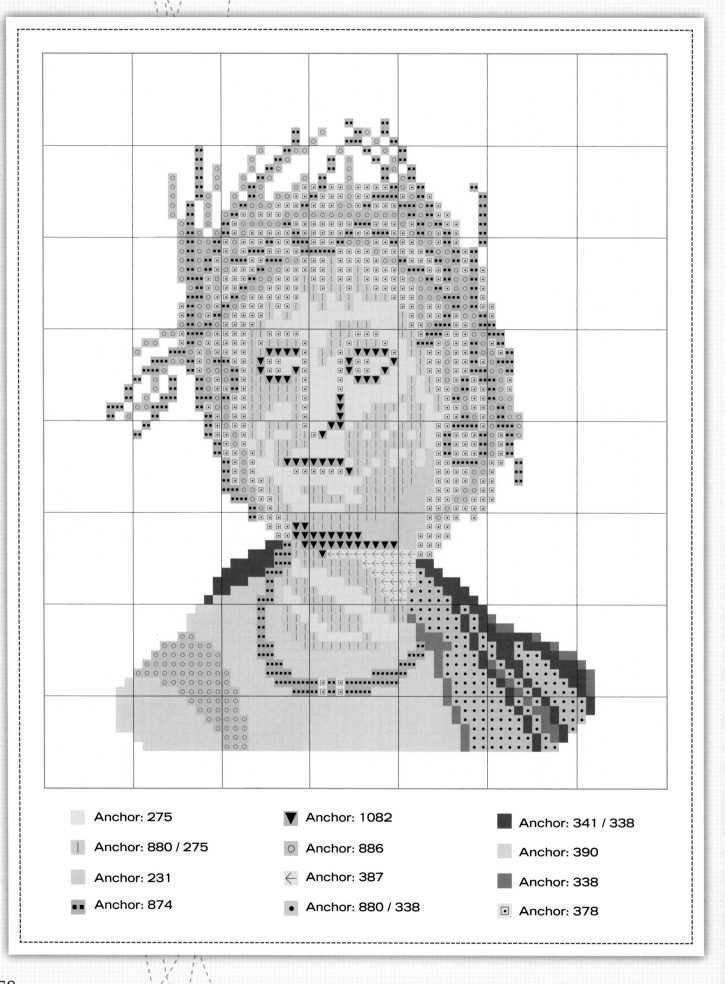

	Anchor: 275	▼	Anchor: 1082		Anchor: 341 / 338
	Anchor: 880 / 275	○	Anchor: 886		Anchor: 390
	Anchor: 231	←	Anchor: 387		Anchor: 338
▪▪	Anchor: 874	•	Anchor: 880 / 338	▣	Anchor: 378

Roman Heads Quilt Plan

This quilt is constructed by working diagonally across rows. This means that the gray diamond blocks can be assembled completely, but the cream ones will only be halves until the completed diagonal rows are stitched together (see page 57).

Use ¼" (6 mm) seam allowances throughout.

Preparing the Patchwork

1. Using tracing paper, make 32 copies of foundation block (A) onto a foundation (see below) to create the gray diamonds.

2. Starting with a dark gray triangle, following the method outlined on page 50, make sixteen pairs of half diamonds with dark sand triangles and sixteen with dark gray triangles.

3. Place a sand and a dark gray half diamond, right sides facing, matching the stitching at the right-angle of each piece to the stitching at the point of the other. The edges of the block will overlap. Stitch the seam right across.

    Press the seam open. You will have a complete gray diamond.

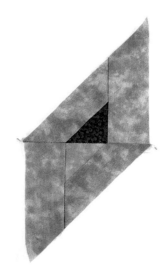

Right Side of Completed Gray Diamond

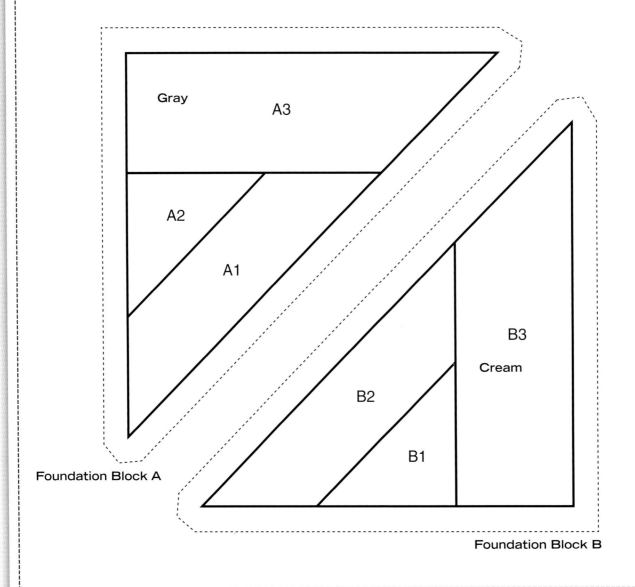

Gray

A3

A2

A1

Foundation Block A

B3

Cream

B2

B1

Foundation Block B

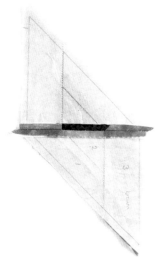

Wrong side of the completed gray diamond

4. Make 32 copies of foundation block B onto a foundation. These are for the cream diamonds. Create 16 pairs of half-diamonds as on page 54, but don't make these into *complete* diamonds.

5. To make the terracotta square units, cut five 3" (7.6 cm) squares from both the light gray and cream center fabrics. Pin a gray and cream square together, right sides together. Draw a diagonal line on the wrong side of the cream fabric. Stitch a ¼" (6 mm) seam on each side of the line, then cut down the drawn line. Press the seam open. You will have two half-square triangle units. Trim to 2½" (6.4 cm). Repeat with the other squares. There will be one spare square.

6. Mark ¼" (6 mm) away from the edges at each corner.

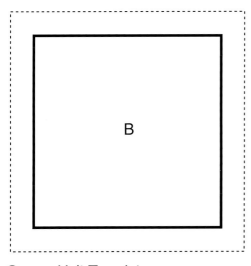

Square Unit Template

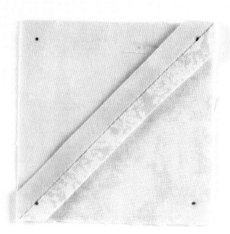

Mark the ¼" (6 mm) points on the completed half-square triangle unit

7. Trace the side template, including the seam line, onto the light and dark terracotta, and cut out 52 side pieces. With right sides together, pin one side piece along the edge of one of the squares. The corners of the square will protrude slightly beyond the side piece. Stitch between the ¼" (6 mm) marks on the square.

8. Repeat with the next side, making sure side 1 is not caught in the stitching. Notice how the adjacent sides share the same marked hole (see also pages 38–39 for Mitered corners).

9. With right sides together, pin the two side pieces together, trapping the folded square between them. Draw a line from the shared stitch along the short side to the edge.

10. Stitch along the line from the shared stitch to the edge.

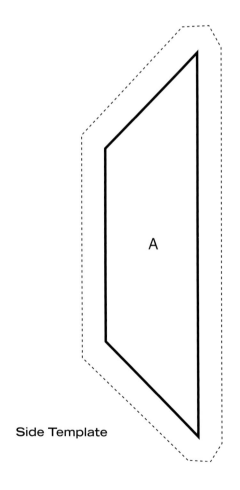

Side Template

A

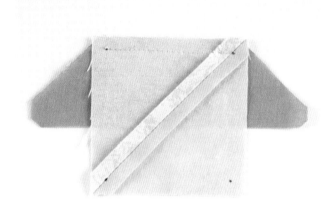

Add a side piece

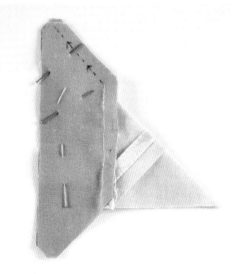

Stitch a miter

11. Open out, finger press, then repeat the procedure adding the remaining side pieces to the square. Press the seams open. You will have a mitered 4½" (11.4 cm) square. You need nine complete squares.

12. Cut four 2½" (6.4 cm) dark gray squares. Cut diagonally to make eight triangles. Add a terra-cotta side piece to the two short sides of each triangle and miter the corner.

13. Cut two 4½" (11.4 cm) gray squares diagonally to form the four corner triangles.

14. Following the quilt plan, start at the top-right corner and stitch the blocks and triangles together in diagonal rows. At the top right-hand corner, it is easier to add the grey corner after the first row has been completed.

The size of the quilt top before adding borders is 22½" × 34½" (57.1 cm × 87.6 cm).

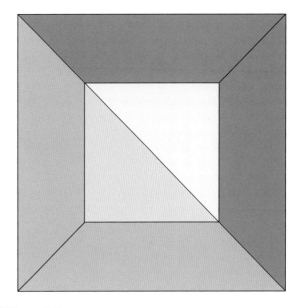

Mitered Square

Mitered Corner

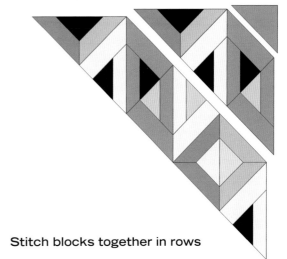

Stitch blocks together in rows

Adding the Borders and Finishing the Quilt

1. Cut two 1¾" × 22½" (4.5 cm × 57.1 cm) gray strips; two 1¾" × 37" (4.5 cm × 94 cm) gray strips; two 2" × 26½" (5.1 cm × 67.3 cm) gray strips; and two 2" × 41½" (5.1 cm × 105.4 cm) gray strips.

2. Cut two 1¼" × 25" (3.2 cm × 63.5 cm) cream strips and two 1¼" × 36½" (3.2 cm × 92.7 cm) cream strips.

3. Stitch a 1¾" × 22½" (4.5 cm × 57.1 cm) gray border to the top and bottom of the quilt. Stitch a 1¾" × 37" (4.5 cm × 94 cm) gray border to each side. Press away from the quilt.

4. Stitch a 1¼" × 25" (3.2 cm × 63.5 cm) cream border to the top and bottom. Press away from the quilt.

5. Stitch a 1¼" × 38½" (3.2 cm × 97.8 cm) cream border to each side.

6. Stitch a 2" × 26½" (5.1 cm × 67.3 cm) gray border to the top and bottom.

7. Stitch a 2" × 41½" (5.1 cm × 105.4 cm) gray border to each side.

8. Make a quilt sandwhich of the backing, batting and top, then quilt. (This quilt was quilted in the ditch around each diamond.) Bind the edges to finish.

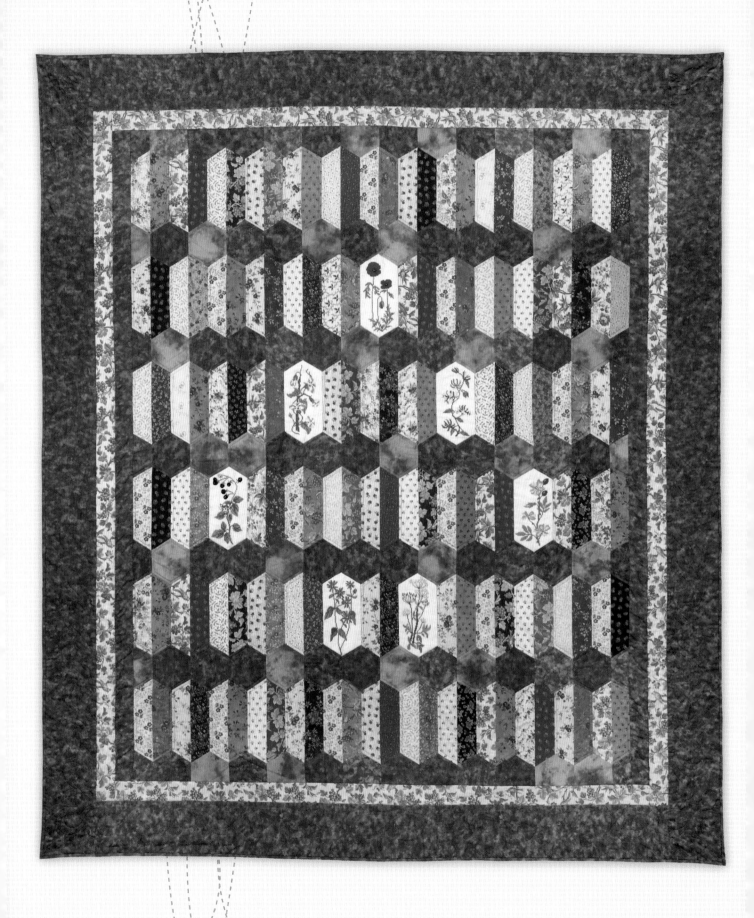

HEDGEROW HEXAGONS

For this project, I used the English method of paper piecing (see page 60). However, as I often like to do, I exercised artistic license and chose to extend the sides of some of the hexagons to form Church Windows. This not only adds visual interest to the quilt, showing off the light and dark fabrics, but the patchwork also grows quickly.

Though you can use any 2½" (6.4 cm) strips of fabric, this is a wonderful project for jelly rolls. I frequently purchase jelly rolls just because I like the color combinations, and this project made great use of my growing surplus! One jelly roll of 40 strips will be sufficient for the long hexagons in this quilt.

The colors of the fabrics are complemented by the colors in the stitched designs, which are all based on flowers found in hedgerows. Some of the tones of the embroidery colors were altered slightly from the authentic colors of the flowers to match those of the fabrics. To select a suitable color range for your project, simply lay threads on your fabric strips and stand back to look at them. Remove any that shout at you.

Materials

FOR THE STITCHING

Seven 10" × 5" (25.4 cm × 12.7 cm) piece of 14-count fabric for each design or 28-count (work over 2 threads)

2 skeins of Anchor embroidery floss in 843

1 skein each of Anchor embroidery floss in 1, 358, 371, 842, 845, 846, 1021, 1022, 1023 and 1025

Small amounts of Anchor embroidery floss in 13, 20, 266, 293, 311, 358, 369, 371, 403, 905 and 1082

FOR THE PATCHWORK

1½ yds. (1.4 m) dark fabric, cut eighteen 2½" (6.4 cm) strips (cut across the width of the fabric) for the long hexagons

1½ yds. (1.4 m) light fabric, cut eighteen 2½" (6.4 cm) strips (cut across the width of the fabric) for the long hexagons

2½ yds. (2.3 m) total of mixed green fabrics, cut ninety-eight 5" × 6" (12.7 cm × 15.2 cm) rectangles for the connecting hexagons

¾ yds. (69 cm) of cream fabric; piece the following:

> two 2½" × 56" (6.4 cm × 142.2 cm) strips for the borders

> two 2½" × 70¼" (6.4 cm × 178.4 cm) strips for the borders

2 yds. (1.8 m) of green fabric; piece the following:

> two 2½" × 66¼" (6.4 cm × 168.3 cm) strips for the borders

> two 6" × 60" (15.2 cm × 152.4 cm) strips for the borders

> two 6" × 82¼" (15.2 cm × 208.9 cm) strips for the borders

Backing and batting, 77" × 87" (195 cm × 221 cm)

Binding, ½ yd. (45.7 cm) 1½" × 310" (3.8 cm × 787.4 cm)

Thin cardstock 60–65 lbs. (100-150 gsm) for the templates

Hedgerow Hexagons
Finished size: 82¼" × 72" (208.9 cm × 182.8 cm)

Grandmother's Flower Garden

Coffin

Church Window

English Paper Piecing

English paper piecing patchwork allows you to join pieces that are irregularly shaped, and thus would be difficult to stitch using a machine. This patchwork technique experienced a revival during the 1920s and 30s and still remains a favorite of hand stitchers today, as shapes such as clam shells and diamonds can be accurately joined by hand using a whip stitch.

Hexagons are a popular shape to stitch using English paper piecing, and the most popular block design is Grandmother's Flower Garden. A central hexagon is surrounded by six others to form a flower shape. Traditionally, the center hexagon is yellow, to represent a flower's center.

Each center is then surrounded by six petals of another color, followed by a ring of green representing grass, and encompassed by a white fence (hence the name Grandmother's Flower Garden). There are numerous variations of the basic design. Sometimes the hexagon colors are extended to create diamond gardens.

Different effects can be achieved by varying the length of the sides of the hexagon. For example, if two parallel sides are extended, the hexagon becomes a Church Window (see above). Conversely, if two angled sides are elongated, the hexagon becomes a Coffin.

Working the Embroidery

1. Using the color keys and charts, stitch the designs in the center of each 10" × 5" (25.4 cm × 12.7 cm) piece of 14-count fabric. (If you use 28-count fabric, work each stitch over the two threads.)

2. Lightly spray with starch and press the back of each embroidery. Then, center the design and cut to a 10" × 5" (25.4 cm × 12.7 cm) rectangle. Pin and baste onto a long hexagon card as described in steps 4–5 on page 69.

Repeat with the other six designs. These are now ready to be incorporated into the patchwork. Refer to the plan on page 68 for placement.

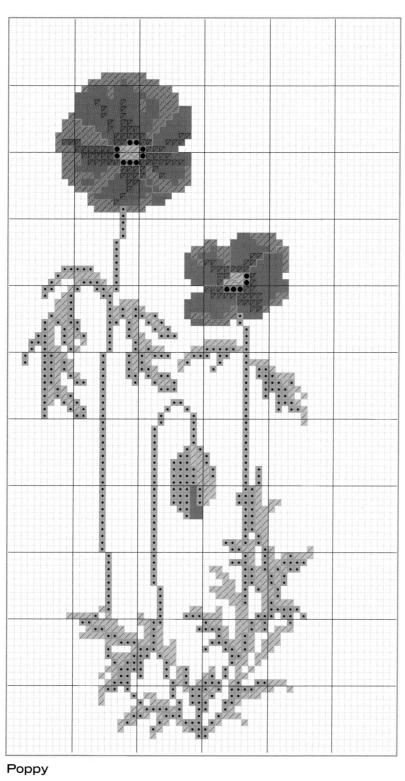

- • Anchor: 843 / 846
- ╱ Anchor: 843
- ◩ Anchor: 20 / 1025
- ╱ Anchor: 13
- ▬ Anchor: 1025
- ● Anchor: 403
- — Anchor: 403

Poppy

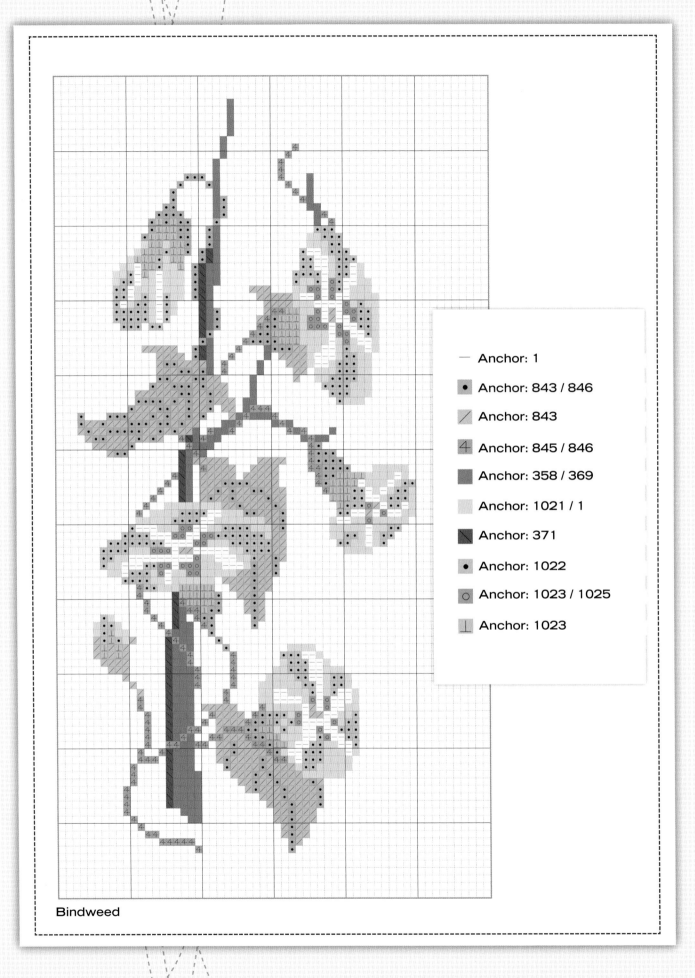

Anchor: 1
Anchor: 843 / 846
Anchor: 843
Anchor: 845 / 846
Anchor: 358 / 369
Anchor: 1021 / 1
Anchor: 371
Anchor: 1022
Anchor: 1023 / 1025
Anchor: 1023

Bindweed

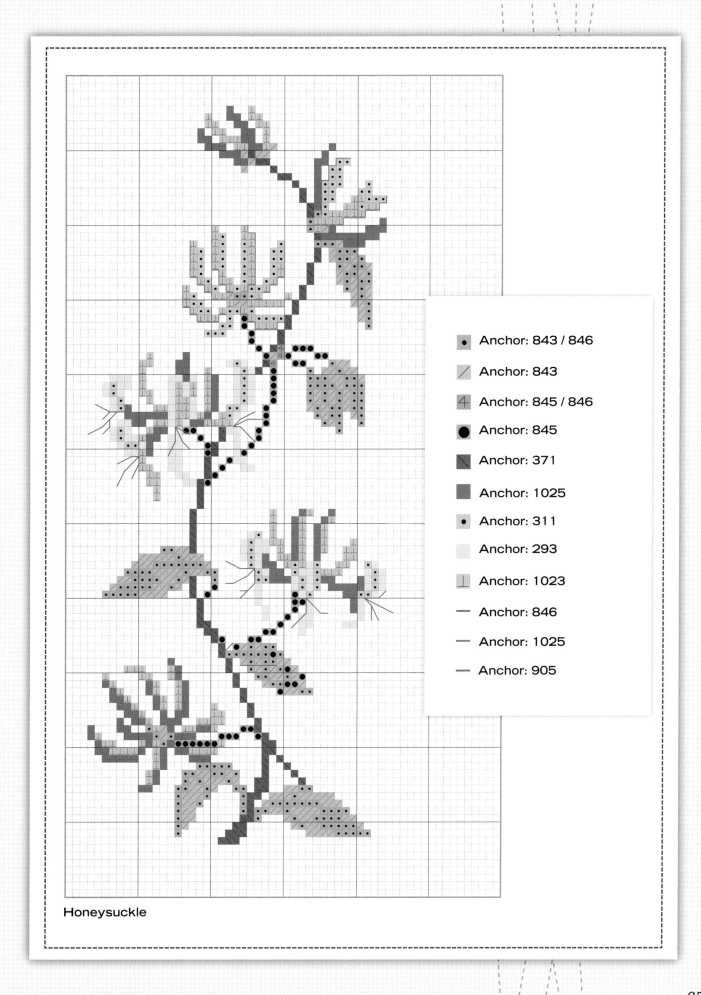

Anchor: 843 / 846

Anchor: 843

Anchor: 845 / 846

Anchor: 845

Anchor: 371

Anchor: 1025

Anchor: 311

Anchor: 293

Anchor: 1023

Anchor: 846

Anchor: 1025

Anchor: 905

Honeysuckle

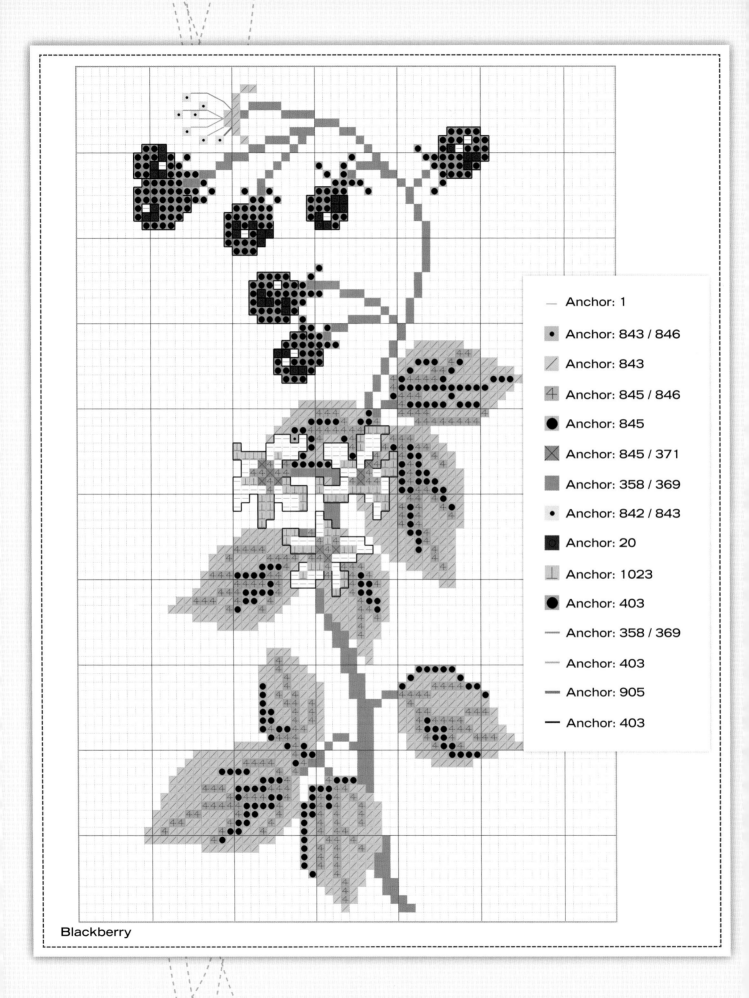

Blackberry

Legend:
- — Anchor: 1
- Anchor: 843 / 846
- Anchor: 843
- Anchor: 845 / 846
- Anchor: 845
- Anchor: 845 / 371
- Anchor: 358 / 369
- Anchor: 842 / 843
- Anchor: 20
- Anchor: 1023
- Anchor: 403
- — Anchor: 358 / 369
- — Anchor: 403
- — Anchor: 905
- — Anchor: 403

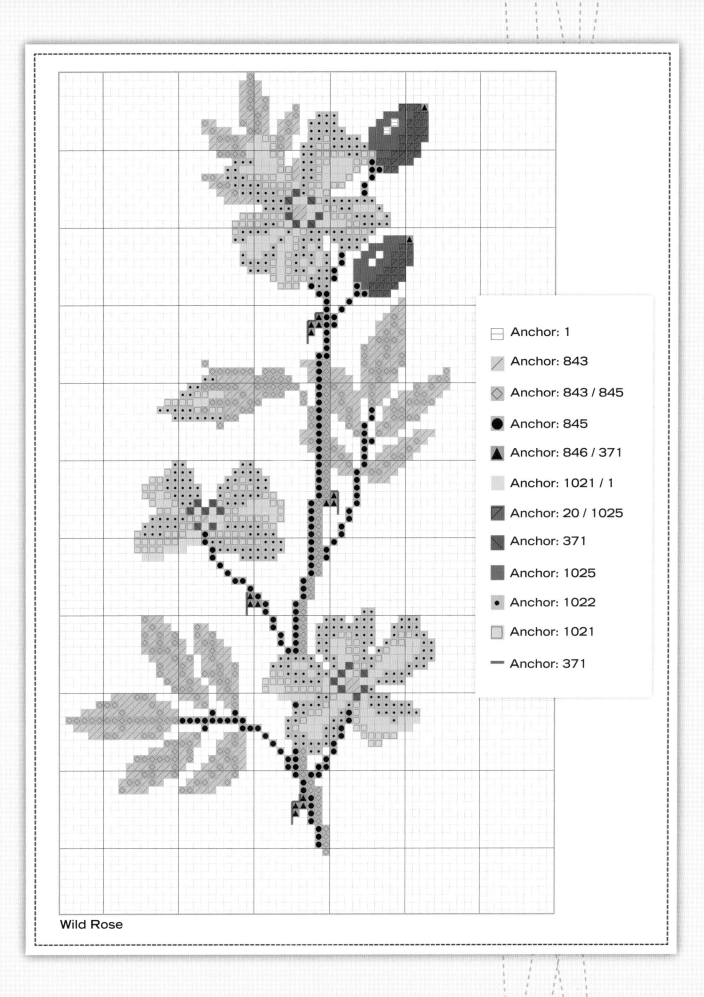

Wild Rose

The legend:

- Anchor: 1
- Anchor: 843
- Anchor: 843 / 845
- Anchor: 845
- Anchor: 846 / 371
- Anchor: 1021 / 1
- Anchor: 20 / 1025
- Anchor: 371
- Anchor: 1025
- Anchor: 1022
- Anchor: 1021
- Anchor: 371

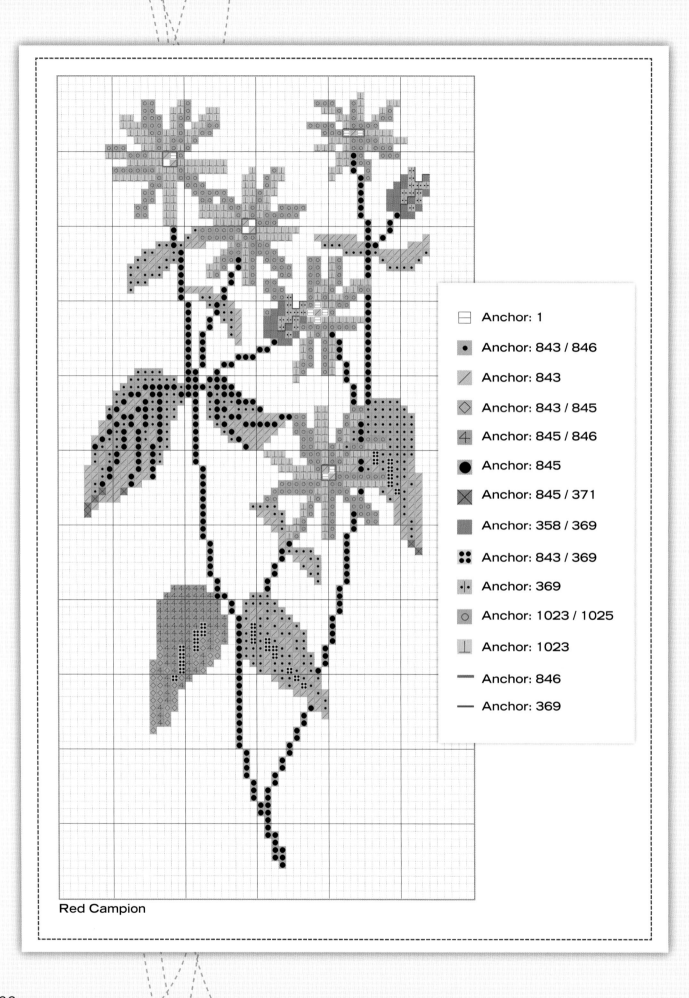

Red Campion

Anchor: 1
Anchor: 843 / 846
Anchor: 843
Anchor: 843 / 845
Anchor: 845 / 846
Anchor: 845
Anchor: 845 / 371
Anchor: 358 / 369
Anchor: 843 / 369
Anchor: 369
Anchor: 1023 / 1025
Anchor: 1023
Anchor: 846
Anchor: 369

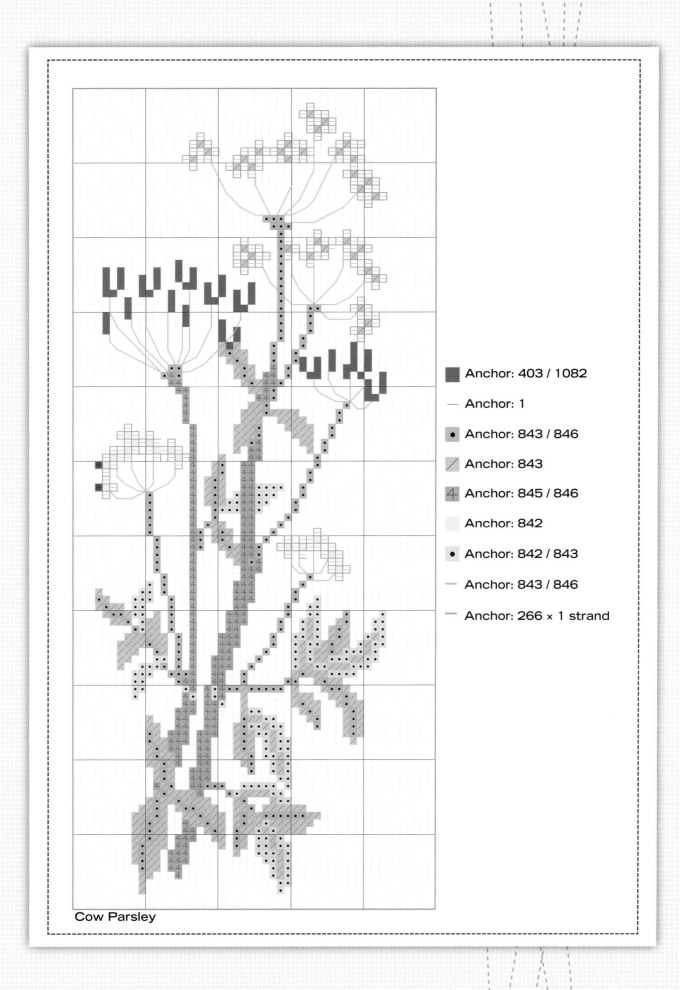

Anchor: 403 / 1082

Anchor: 1

Anchor: 843 / 846

Anchor: 843

Anchor: 845 / 846

Anchor: 842

Anchor: 842 / 843

Anchor: 843 / 846

Anchor: 266 × 1 strand

Cow Parsley

Hedgerow Hexagons Quilt Plan

You will use English paper piecing for this patchwork project. The embroidery designs are: 1. Poppy, 2. Bindweed, 3.Honeysuckle, 4. Blackberry, 5. Wild Rose, 6. Red Campion and 7. Cow Parsley.

Use a ¼" (6 mm) seam allowance throughout.

Preparing the Patchwork

1. Join the light and dark 2½" (6.4 cm) strips for the long hexagons together in pairs to form the strip sets and press the seams open. For more variation in the color combinations, you can cut strips in half and mix them up before joining them together.

2. Cut the strip sets crosswise into 10" (25.4 cm) lengths. You will have four 4½" × 10" (11.4 cm × 25.4 cm) pieces from each long strip. If you cut the strips in half before joining them, you will have two pieces from each combination.

3. Trace the long hexagon template onto paper. Glue this to a firm piece of cardstock and cut it out carefully. Trace this template onto thin cardstock to make 78 hexagons.

4. Make 71 bi-colored hexagons. Pin the card template in the center of the wrong side of the fabric, making sure that the points are exactly in line with the center seam. Trim to leave a ¼" (6 mm) excess fabric all round. Fold the fabric over the card and baste to hold it in place. This tacking will be removed later so doesn't need to be perfect.

5. Trace the regular hexagon template on the green fabric, and cut out allowing a ¼" (6 mm) seam allowance. Repeat to make 98 regular green hexagons.

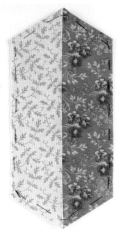

Finished Long Hexagon (Front)

Finished Long Hexagon (Back)

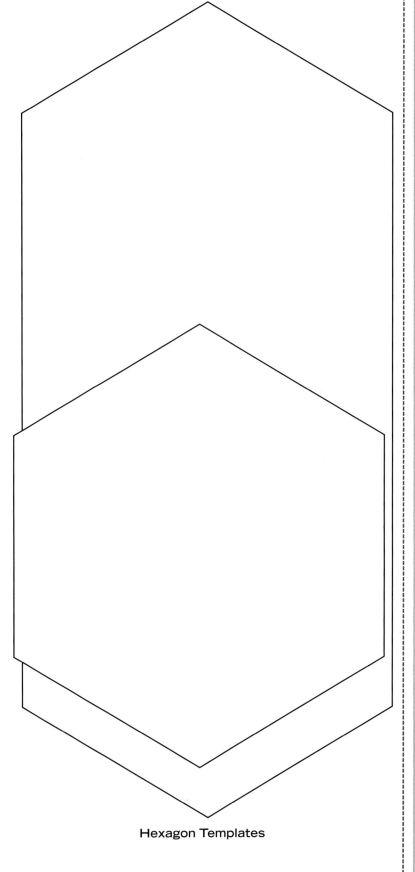

Hexagon Templates

Making the Quilt Top

1. Arrange the long hexagons and embroidery into six rows of 13.

2. Arrange the regular hexagons into seven rows of 14. If the greens are varied, arrange them with the long hexagons to see the whole quilt plan.

3. Number each hexagon and each row in order on the card, then bundle the hexagons in each numbered row together with an elastic band. This makes it easy to pick up and stitch individual rows without having to lay them out again.

4. Overcast the long sides of complete rows of long hexagons together, including the embroidery. Use small stitches and start and finish each with a double stitch. Slide the needle to catch the two fabric pieces avoiding sewing through the card.

   When all the rows are complete, stitch the rows together, keeping the card in place. Don't worry if the card becomes creased as you manipulate the hexagons; this won't affect your quilt top.

5. When the top is complete, keep the cards in place and press the back. Then, lightly spray the top with starch and press well. To finish, remove the cards by taking out the tacking. The card templates should come out easily. Press the patchwork a final time.

6. Open out the folded seams on the quilt sides and press gently, leaving a clear line for placing the border. The fold line is the line for the stitching, and the fabric that was folded around the card becomes the ¼" (6 mm) seam allowance.

   Lay the opened edges of the regular hexagons over the top of the long hexagons.

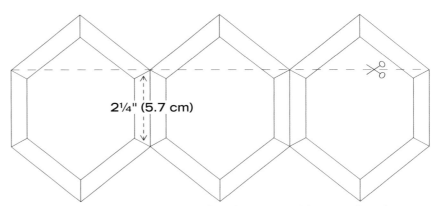

2¼" (5.7 cm)

Prepare the opened-out edges for the top and bottom borders

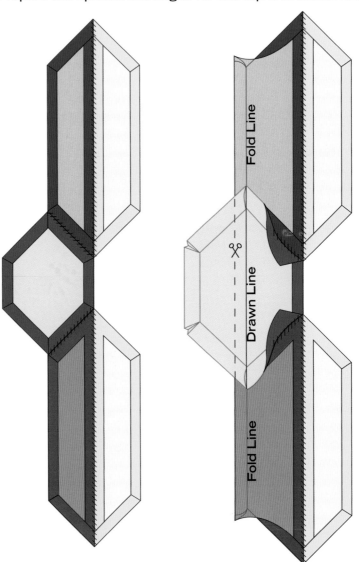

Fold Line

Fold Line

Drawn Line

Fold Line

Prepare the side edges for the borders

On the back of the regular hexagons, draw a line connecting the fold lines of the long hexagons. This is the stitching line. Cut off the excess fabric, allowing a ¼" (6 mm) seam allowance. You now have a straight edge to attach the border.

Piecing a Border or Binding Length

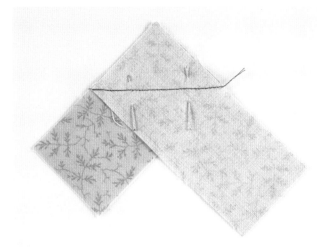

Figure A

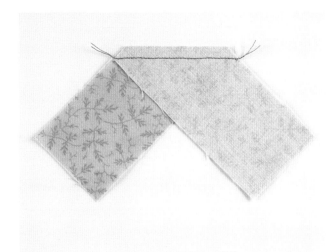

Figure B

Adding the Borders and Finishing the Quilt

1. To piece a border or binding length, take two strips of fabric cut to the border or binding width. Place them right sides together on top of each other at right angles to form a V. Stitch diagonally across the strips. (Figure A) Trim the seam to ¼" (6 mm). (Figure B) Press open. Cut off the dog-ears level with the edge. (Figures C)

2. Pin and stitch one 2½" × 66¼" (6.4 cm × 168.3 cm) green border to each side of the quilt top.

3. Draw a line across the back of the green hexagons at the top and bottom of the quilt 2¼" (6.4 cm) from the point of the long hexagon. Cut along the line. This forms a green border to match the sides.

4. Pin and stitch a 2½" × 56" (6.4 cm × 142.2 cm) cream border to the top and bottom, press open. Then pin and stitch a 2½" × 70¼" (6.4 cm × 178.4 cm) cream border to each side, and press open.

5. Add a 6" × 60" (15.2 cm × 152.4 cm) green border to the top and bottom, then add a 6" × 82¼" (15.2 cm × 208.9 cm) green border to each side.

6. Put the top, batting and backing together to form the quilt sandwich. Then quilt as you wish.

7. Add a 1½" (3.8 cm) binding to complete the quilt.

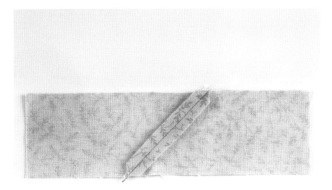

Figure C: Wrong side of fabric

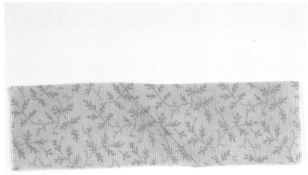

Figure C: Right side of fabric

EDWARD BEAR

My grandson Stephen was born while I was preparing this book, so I decided to create an embroidered wall hanging to celebrate the special occasion. I stitched Edward Bear and the personalized information, but I wasn't yet satisfied with the piece. The addition of a wide border with quilted stars in plaid fabrics that complemented the embroidery gave the wall hanging that extra special touch I was looking for. If just the stitching had been framed and hung on the wall, it wouldn't have had quite the same impact.

The accompanying CD contains a chart for the bear design on plain graph paper as well as charts for the alphabet in both upper and lowercase. By substituting your own text and perhaps another stitched design, you could easily adapt this quilted wall hanging for a birthday, anniversary or any other special occasion.

Edward Bear
Finished size: 17½" × 14½" (44.5 cm × 36.8 cm)

Materials

FOR THE STITCHERY

13" × 10" (33 cm × 25.4 cm) piece of antique white 14-count Aida (work over every thread) or 28-count evenweave (work over two threads)

1 skein each of Anchor Embroidery floss in 887, 888 and 1006

Small amount Anchor of Anchor 45, 372, 403, 886, 885, 889, 1352 and white (used for a highlight in each eye)

Cream Perlé 8 for embroidered hearts

FOR THE PATCHWORK

⅜ yd (34 cm) beige/cream fabric; cut the following:

> two 1½" × 15½" (3.8 cm × 39.3 cm) strips for borders
>
> two 1½" × 12½" (3.8 cm × 31.8 cm) strips for borders
>
> four 1¼" (3.2 cm) squares and four 2" (5.1 cm) squares for each star block

¼ yd (22.9 cm) plaid fabric; cut the following:

> five 2" (5.1 cm) squares of plaid for each of the 14 blocks
>
> three 2" (5.1 cm) squares of plaid for the hearts

¼ yd (22.9 cm) red fabric; cut the following:

> four 1½" (3.8 cm) squares
>
> Binding, approximately 1½" × 66" (3.8 cm × 167.6 cm) of fabric

Batting and backing, 19" × 23" (48.3 cm × 58.4 cm)

14 buttons (optional)

Fusible web for hearts

Tracing paper or template plastic for embroidered heart templates

Working the Embroidery

1. First, plan your writing. Use graph paper and a pencil with an eraser, making adjustments as needed.

2. Follow the color chart and key to stitch the design in the correct place on the fabric. Count the squares on the plan. The central panel is 9" × 6" (22.9 cm × 15.2 cm). It may be useful to mark the edges of the design area, shown here in red, with basting. This will help you with the placement of the three hearts. There is excess fabric to allow for slight errors. Note that there are places you will need to thread your needle with two different colors, one strand of each.

3. Trace the larger heart three times onto the paper side of the fusible webbing. Cut these hearts out roughly and iron onto the back of the chosen fabrics. Cut them out carefully, peel off the backing and iron them where you like onto the Aida or evenweave in the space below the date. Stitch around them in blanket stitch or couch the edges (see page 93).

4. When the design is complete, lightly spray with starch and press on the wrong side. Cut to 9½" × 6½" (24.1 cm × 16.5 cm). You may find it better to delay cutting until you are ready to make up the quilt top to prevent fraying.

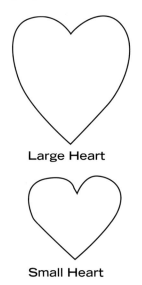

Large Heart

Small Heart

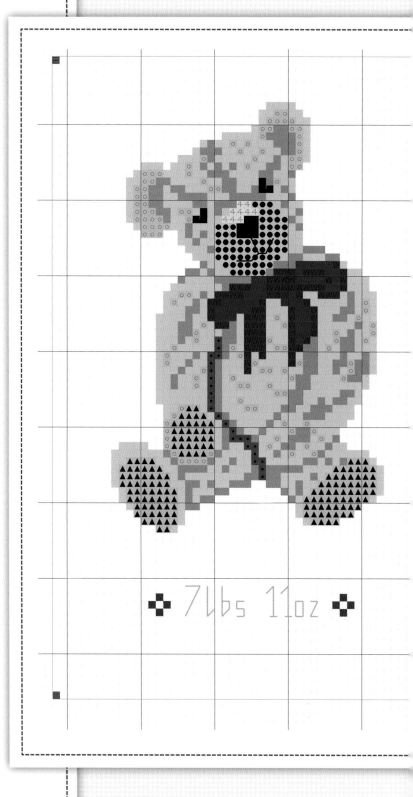

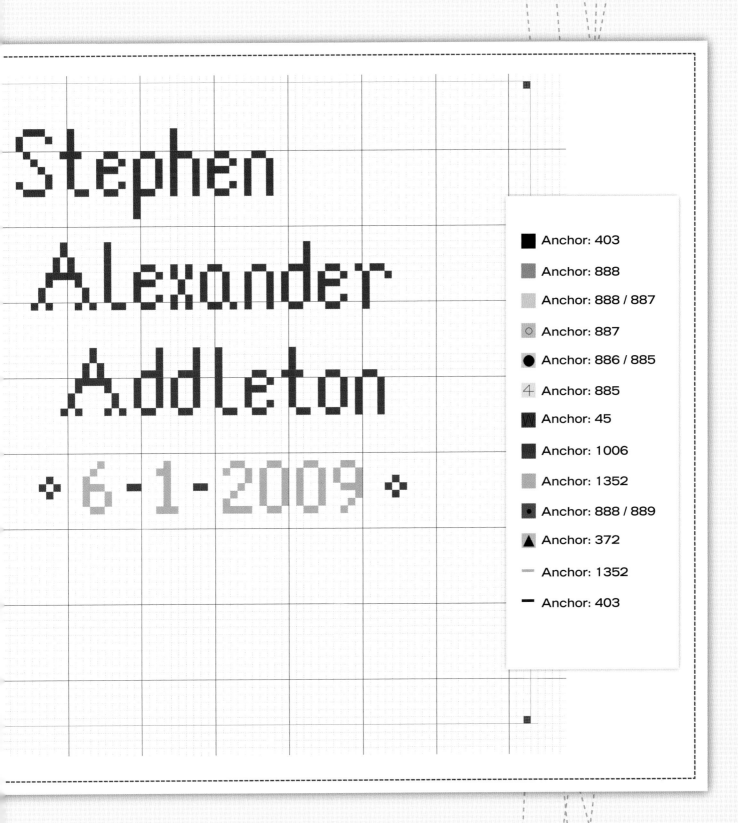

Stephen
Alexander
Addleton
❖ 6-1-2009 ❖

■	Anchor: 403
▓	Anchor: 888
▒	Anchor: 888 / 887
○	Anchor: 887
●	Anchor: 886 / 885
4	Anchor: 885
W	Anchor: 45
■	Anchor: 1006
▮	Anchor: 1352
•	Anchor: 888 / 889
▲	Anchor: 372
−	Anchor: 1352
−	Anchor: 403

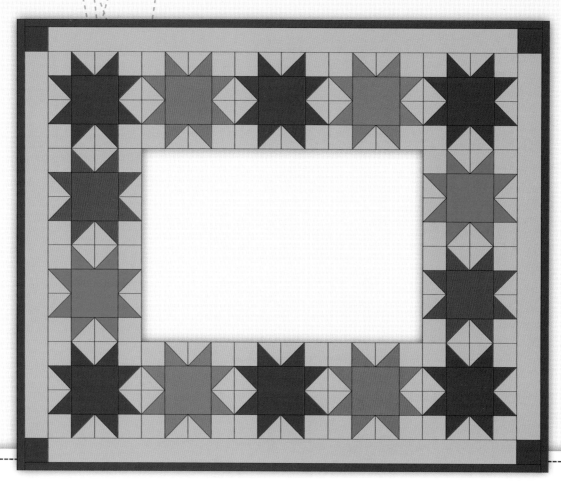

Edward Bear Quilt Plan

Because I made this wall hanging for a boy, I chose plaid fabrics in darker colors.

Use ¼" (6 mm) seam allowances throughout. Each finished block measures 3" (7.6 cm).

ALTERING THE PALETTE TO SUIT YOUR NEEDS

If you'd like to make this quilt for a young girl, you may choose to use a more traditionally feminine palette of pastel pinks and purples. You might also prefer to select fabrics with floral prints, polka dots or stars instead of the plaids that I used.

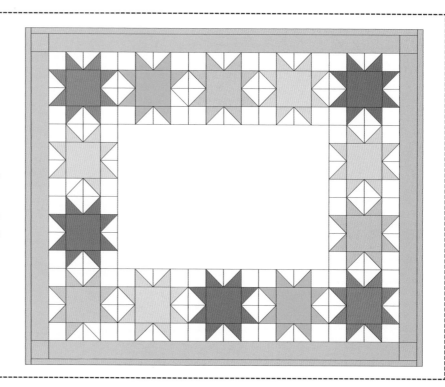

Making the Star Blocks

1. Cut four 1¼" (3.2 cm) squares and four 2" (5.1 cm) squares from cream fabric, and cut five 2" (5.1 cm) squares from one plaid fabric. Stitch the four 2" (5.1 cm) cream squares and four of the 2" (5.1 cm) plaid squares together to make eight half-square triangle units (see half-square triangle units on page 32). Trim them to 1¼" (3.2 cm) square.

2. Following the block plan, stitch the half-square triangle units in pairs, with the cream forming a triangle. Stitch a half-square triangle pair to opposite sides of the 2" (5.1 cm) plaid squares. This is the middle section.

3. Stitch a 1¼" (3.2 cm) cream square to each side of the remaining two half-square triangle pairs.

4. Following the plan, stitch one of these at the top and one at the bottom of the middle section to make a star. Trim to 3½" (8.9 cm) square, then press. Make a total of 14 colored star blocks.

Making the Quilt Top

1. Trace the small heart onto paper. Glue the paper to a piece of cardstock or template plastic, then carefully cut it out to make a template for the embroidered hearts.

   Trace the template onto each star using an erasable marking pen. Then stitch the outline with cream perlé cotton using a backstitch. Add a French knot or bead.

2. Arrange the stars, then stitch five together side by side for the top row and five for the bottom row, matching seams carefully. Make sure all the hearts are positioned the same way. Stitch the other four stars in pairs one above the other for the sides, as shown.

3. Pin and stitch one side pair of stars at each side of the embroidery. Taking care to match the seams, pin and stitch the top and bottom rows of stars to the embroidery. Trim to 12½" × 15½" (31.8 cm × 39.4 cm).

Adding the Borders and Finishing the Quilt

1. Stitch a 1½" × 15½" (3.8 cm × 39.3 cm) cream strip to the top and bottom of the quilt center.

2. Stitch a 1½" (3.8 cm) red square at each end of a 1½" × 12½" (3.8 cm × 31.8 cm) cream strip. Pin and stitch this to one side of the quilt center, matching the seams. Repeat for the other side.

3. Make the quilt sandwich, then quilt. Bind the edges.

4. Stitch a button on each connecting diamond, if desired.

Star Block Plan

Arrangement of Star Blocks

BLUE FLORAL DELIGHT

This dramatic quilt is the result of alternating a nine-patch block with a design stitched on calico. And, my, what a pleasure it was to make!

A variety of clear, simplified flower designs—similar to botanical drawings—contrast nicely with the simple nine-patch blocks. The addition of short Victorian poems about flowers creates even more visual interest. Simply follow the instructions in this project to add the poems or sayings of your choice. As an added bonus, the stitchery pieces are portable projects that can easily can be slipped in a bag and taken with you wherever you go.

The color scheme for this project was inspired by the variegated colors of the thread—a rich blue and purple mix—and the fact that I had lots of small pieces of fabric in similar colors. You could use any dark variegated thread and a coordinating range of colors for the nine-patch blocks. As the design requires squares of only 2½" (6.3 cm), and any number of colors can be employed, take the opportunity to use up lots of scraps—the more the merrier! Alternative block designs include variations on Snowball or Bright Hopes Twist. The amount of fabric needed may vary if you choose to replace the nine-patch block with another design.

Materials

FOR THE STITCHERY

7 skeins DMC 4240 embroidery floss

FOR THE PATCHWORK

Three-hundred and seventy-two 2½" (6.3 cm × 6.3 cm) squares of assorted purples and blues (184 purple, 184 blue) for nine-patch squares and pieced middle border. This is approximately 1 yd. (.9 m) total of several purple fabrics, and 1 yd. (.9 m) total of several blue fabrics

¼ yd. (22.9 cm) light fabric for nine-patch centers

1½ yds. (1.4 m) lightweight cream/off white calico for the embroidery

2 yds. (1.8 m) border fabric; cut the following:

> two 3¾" × 69" (9.5 cm × 179.3 cm) strips (to be cut lengthwise to avoid piecing) for sides of outer border
>
> two 3¾" × 50½" (9.5 cm × 128.3 cm) strips (to be cut lengthwise to avoid piecing) for top and bottom of outer border
>
> two 2½" × 58½" (6.3 cm × 148.6 cm) strips (to be cut lengthwise to avoid piecing) for sides of inner border
>
> two 2½" × 42½" (6.3 cm × 102.9 cm) strips (to be cut lengthwise to avoid piecing) for top and bottom of inner border
>
> four 2½" (6.3 cm) squares for border ends
>
> as many 2½" (6.3 cm) squares as you can cut from remaining fabric to be included in nine-patch units and pieced border

Backing and batting, 62" × 74" (157.5 cm × 188 cm)

Binding, ⅜ yd. (34.3 cm) blue fabric to make a strip 1½" × 250" (3.8 cm × 635 cm)

Thirty-two buttons of your choice for the nine-patch squares (optional)

Blue Floral Delight
Finished size: 57" x 69" (144.8 cm x 175.3 cm)

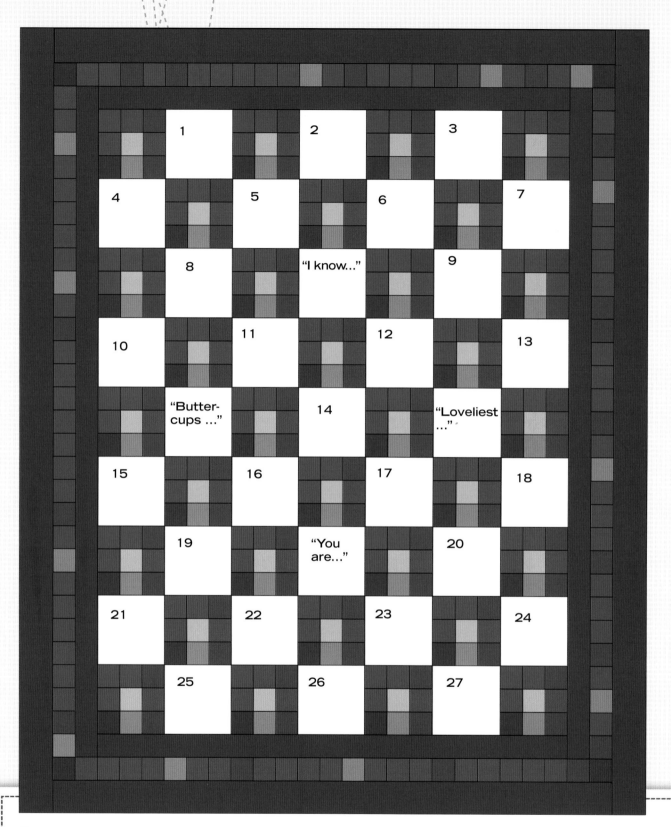

Blue Floral Delight Quilt Plan

The numbers listed above correspond to the 27 floral designs on the next two pages.

Choose a batting that can be ironed, as the calico squares may need a final press after the quilt is complete.

Use ¼" (6 mm) seam allowances throughout. Each finished block measures 6" × 6" (15.2 cm × 15.2 cm).

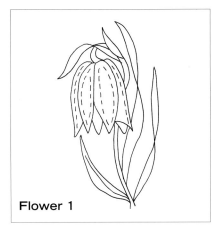

Flower 1

Flower 2

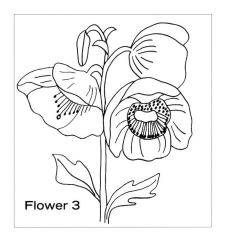

Flower 3

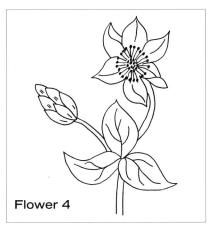

Flower 4

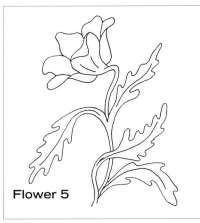

Flower 5

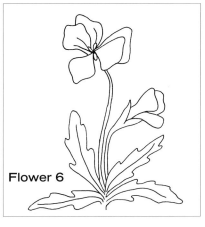

Flower 6

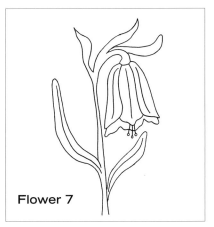

Flower 7

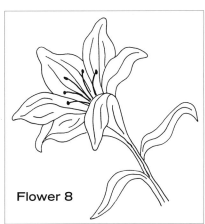

Flower 8

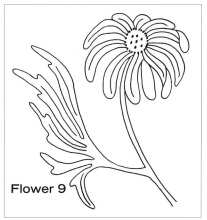

Flower 9

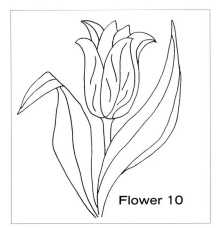

Flower 10

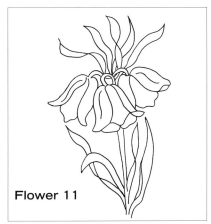

Flower 11

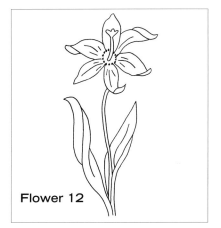

Flower 12

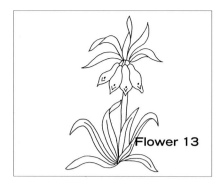

Flower 13

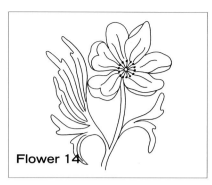

Flower 14

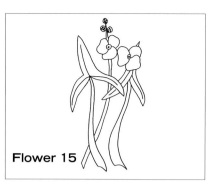

Flower 15

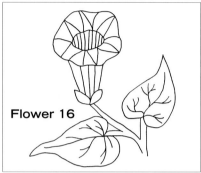

Flower 16

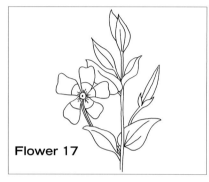

Flower 17

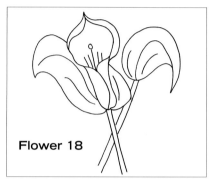

Flower 18

Flower 19

Flower 20

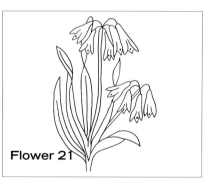

Flower 21

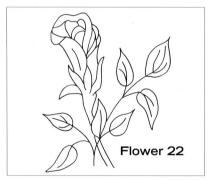

Flower 22

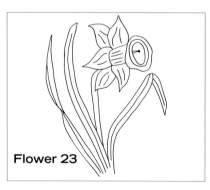

Flower 23

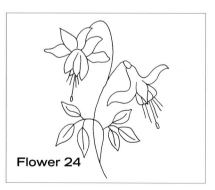

Flower 24

Flower 25

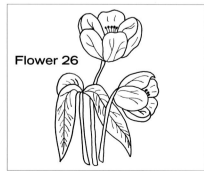

Flower 26

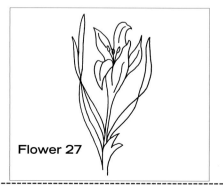

Flower 27

Transferring the Designs Onto the Calico

1. Enlarge the design to the size that you need using a copier. The finished blocks for this quilt need to be 6" (15.24 cm). If you don't have access to a copier, first draw a light pencil grid of 1" (2.5 cm) squares over the design plan. Then, on a separate piece of paper, draw a grid of 2" (5 cm) squares. Draw the design square by square, copying from the original.

   If you require a different increase or decrease of the pattern, vary the size of square proportionately, For example, for half the original size, draw ½" (0.75 cm) squares, or for three times the size, draw 3" (7.5 cm) squares.

2. Cut the calico into thirty-one 8" (20 cm) squares.

   Transfer each design onto the center of a calico square. To do this, pin or tape the enlarged paper design beneath the calico, hold it against a window or use a lightbox, and trace the design onto the calico If the paper design is not clearly visible through onto the calico, go over the lines on the paper with a black marker. I use a silver marking pencil, as I find the pencil marks gradually disappear as the quilt is handled. However, other fabric markers are available that will either wash or brush out. Follow the individual manufacturer's directions to remove guidelines when you are done stitching.

Embroidering the Designs

1. Unless otherwise stated, use two strands is used for stemstitching the main stems and outlines, and use one strand for stemstitching the veins and petal markings. Where appropriate, use French knots for the centers of the flowers.

   Follow the stitches indicated for the other features. See page 11 for stitch instructions.

2. Once the stitching is complete, Press the piece on the wrong side. You may find it useful to spray the fabric with starch first, which adds body and helps prevent fraying. Trim the square to 6½" (17.2 cm), making sure the design is centered.

Enlarging a Design

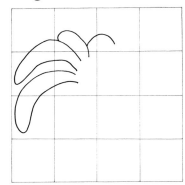

Transferring a Design

Finished Embroidery

Preparing Text for the Poems

1. The text shown here is on the CD for you to print, along with alternatives, but you may wish to use your own text. In this case, first select the short poems or sayings that you would like to include in your quilt. The easiest way to create a template to trace onto the calico is compose it on a computer. For this demonstration, I used Microsoft Paint, but you can use any graphics or art program. Use a clear, simple font for ease of stitching. I selected Times New Roman size 36 for these poems, but I simplified some of the lettering for stitching.

2. As the size of the block can't be any larger than 6" (15 cm), set the page Attributes. (This feature is often found through *Image*, then *Attributes* to that size. Type *Attributes* in Help if you can't locate it.) Type your text using your chosen font and arrange it to your liking. It will print to the required size.

3. Select Bold for the text and print it out. Then transfer the lettering to the calico as for the flower designs (page 83).

4. Stitch the text using either a close stem stitch or a small backstitch. Use a French knot for dots.

Creating Lettering for the Stitching

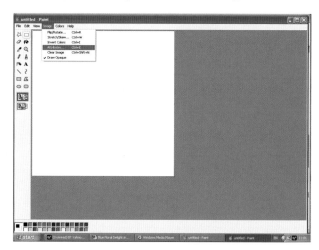

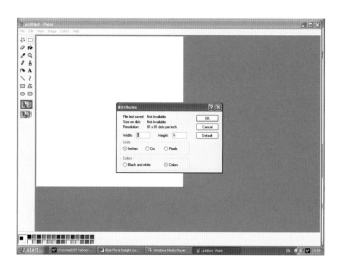

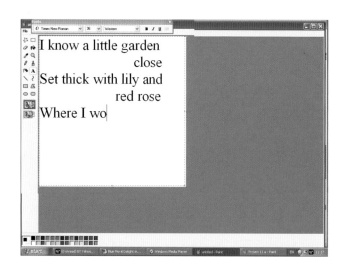

I know a little garden
close
Set thick with lily and
red rose
Where I would wander
if I might
From dewy dawn to
dewy night

Finished Embroidery

Making the Nine-Patch Blocks

1. Cut all of the fabrics for the nine-patch squares and sort them into three piles: blues, purples and centers.

   Take three different blues and join them to make a strip. Do the same with three purples. Make another strip with one blue, one center and one purple. Don't press the seams at this stage. Repeat this procedure until you have 32 strips in each pile.

2. Take one strip from each pile and arrange them to make a nine-patch block. The blue and purple squares in the center strip should be in the same places for each nine-patch block.

   Press the seams of the blue strip and purple strip up, and the seams of the center strip down to make the seams fit together snugly. Join the three strips to make a nine-patch block.

3. Press the two vertical seams away from the center of the nine-patch block. If necessary, trim to 6½" (17.2 cm). Make 31 more nine-patch blocks.

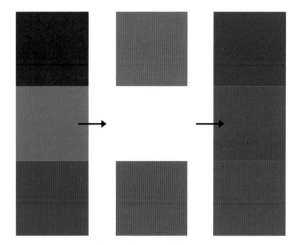

Assembling a Nine-Patch Block

Making the Quilt Top

1. Arrange the 9-patch blocks and embroidered squares to your liking. Pin then stitch the seven blocks for row 1 together. Pressing from the front, press the seams all the same direction.

2. Do the same with row 2, but press the seams in the opposite direction. This will allow the seams to fit neatly against each other as on the nine-patch blocks.

3. Pin and stitch row 3, pressing the seams in the same direction as row 1. Continue in the same way until all the rows are complete, alternating seam direction every row.

4. Taking care to match the seams, stitch the rows together. Press the seams to one side from the front.

Adding the Borders and Finishing the Quilt

1. Pin and stitch the 2½" × 42½" (6.3 cm × 102.9 cm) border strips to the top edge of the quilt and one to the bottom. Pin the two ends of each length first, then ease the quilt top to fit, and press toward the borders. Pin, stitch and press open the 2½" × 58½" (6.3 cm × 148.6 cm) border strips to the sides in the same way.

2. For the second border, retrieve the 2½" (6.3 cm) squares. Keeping aside four squares of border fabric, sew two strips of 23 assorted purples and blues. Pin and stitch these to the top and bottom of the quilt and press toward border 1.

   Now make two strips of 29 squares, and then add a border square at each end, making 31 pieces altogether. Pin and stitch these to the two sides of the quilt and press toward border 1.

3. Pin and stitch the outer border strips to the top, bottom and sides of the quilt.

4. Make the quilt sandwich of the backing, batting and top. Quilt in the ditch around the calico squares. Add any other quilting you wish to the nine-patches and borders. Being careful not to cut the binding fabric, trim the batting and backing to measure 62" × 74" (157.5 cm × 188 cm). Finish binding the quilt.

FLOWERS IN ART

I find the different styles of art that have developed throughout the world fascinating. The designs in this quilt are based not only on paintings, but on textiles, architecture, wallpaper, ceramics and manuscripts as well.

Although the original plan was to have black letters, I used a dark gray instead, as this gave a softer look on the antique white evenweave. I worked the stitching using a single thread for the same reason.

The appliqué patches could be replaced by two of the 5½" (14 cm) blocks. Likewise, if the quilt is to be used as a wall hanging, you could substitute gold thread for the yellow 298.

Because the letter charts could fill up a book by themselves, I've included only the charts for A and Z here. The rest of the charts can be found on the accompanying CD in black-and-white symbol formats for your printing convenience. The small pictures included show all the designs with their origins in the correct coloring. Note that the charts are prepared for ease of working and may not be colored correctly.

Materials

FOR THE STITCHERY

Twenty-six 8" (20 cm) squares of antique white 28-count evenweave or 14-count Aida

5 skeins of Anchor embroidery floss in 236 and 400

2 skeins of Anchor embroidery floss in 843

1 skein each of Anchor embroidery floss in 22, 74, 76, 78, 87, 110, 112, 129, 147, 149, 279, 281, 297, 298, 307, 309, 316, 352, 386, 842, 845, 846, 858, 860, 861, 872, 873, 895, 1012, 1019 and 5975

Small amounts of Anchor embroidery floss in 108, 109, 140, 335, 337, 341, 870, 893, 896, 903 and 924

FOR THE APPLIQUÉ

Wonder Under or an alternative fusible web for appliqué

Air-erasable or removable marking pencil

Sharp pencil

Embroidery floss to match the appliqué fabrics

FOR THE PATCHWORK

2½ yds. (2.3 m) cream fabric; cut the following (lengthwise):

> four 2½" × 66" (6.4 cm × 167.6 cm) strips
>
> four 2" × 43" (5.1 cm × 109 cm) strips
>
> four 3½" × 14¾" (8.9 cm × 37.5 cm) rectangles
>
> four 3½" × 4¾" (8.9 cm × 12.1 cm) rectangles
>
> sixty-six 2¼" × 6" (5.7 cm × 15.2 cm) rectangles
>
> sixty-six 1¼" × 2½" (3.2 cm × 6.4 cm) rectangles
>
> two 9" × 15" (22.8 cm × 38 cm) rectangles for appliqué

½ yd. (54.7 cm) dark red fabric; cut the following:

> thirty-three 1½" × 4½" (3.8 cm × 11.4 cm) strips
>
> four 1½" × 21" (3.8 cm × 53.3 cm) strips
>
> two 3½" × 7½" (8.9 cm × 19 cm) rectangles
>
> two 2½" × 5" (6.4 cm × 12.7 cm) rectangles
>
> two 2½" × 2¾" (6.4 cm × 7 cm) rectangles

½ yd. (45.7 cm) mixed gold fabrics; cut the following:

> four 1½" × 21" (3.8 cm × 53.3 cm) strips
>
> two 2½" × 2¾" (6.4 cm × 7 cm), and two 2½" × 5 ¼" (6.4 cm × 13.3 cm) from the same color for the corners
>
> two 3½" × 7½" (8.9 cm × 19 cm) rectangles
>
> two 1½" × 4½" (3.8 cm × 11.4 cm) rectangles

¼ yd. (22.9 cm) green for seven 1½" × 4½" (3.8 cm × 11.4 cm) rectangles

Seventy-eight 2½" (6.4 cm) squares of assorted oranges, yellows, reds and greens for the border

Small amount of brown for the branches of appliqué

Batting and backing, 60" × 70" (152.5 cm × 178 cm)

Binding, ⅜ yd. (34.3 cm) for approximately 1½" × 244" (3.8 cm × 620 cm)

Flowers in Art
Finished size: 65½" × 54½" (166.4 cm × 138.4 cm)

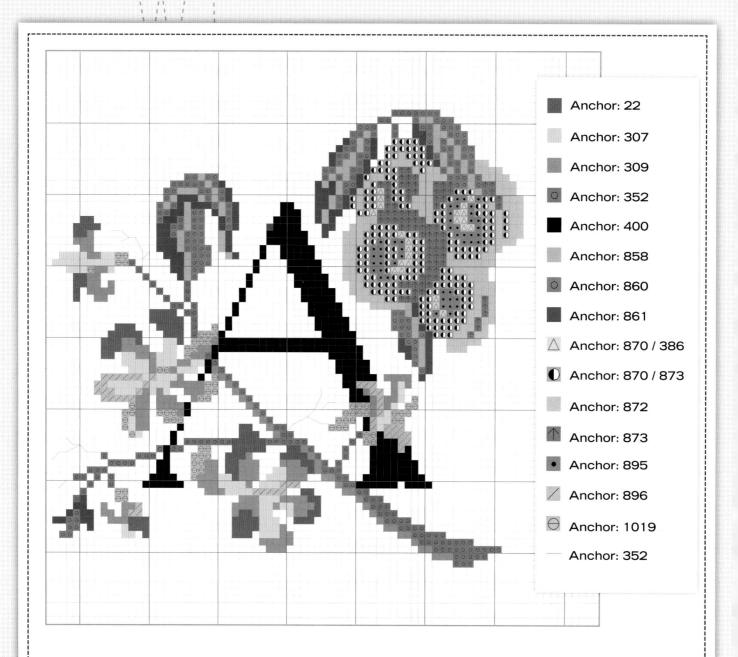

Anchor: 22
Anchor: 307
Anchor: 309
Anchor: 352
Anchor: 400
Anchor: 858
Anchor: 860
Anchor: 861
Anchor: 870 / 386
Anchor: 870 / 873
Anchor: 872
Anchor: 873
Anchor: 895
Anchor: 896
Anchor: 1019
Anchor: 352

Working the Embroidery

1. Following the charts and color keys, embroider the designs in the centers of the 8" (20 cm) squares in cross-stitch and backstitch. Use two strands of gray for the letters and a single strand for all other stitching.

2. When the designs are complete, spray lightly with starch on the wrong side and press. Trim each to 6" (15.24 cm) square.

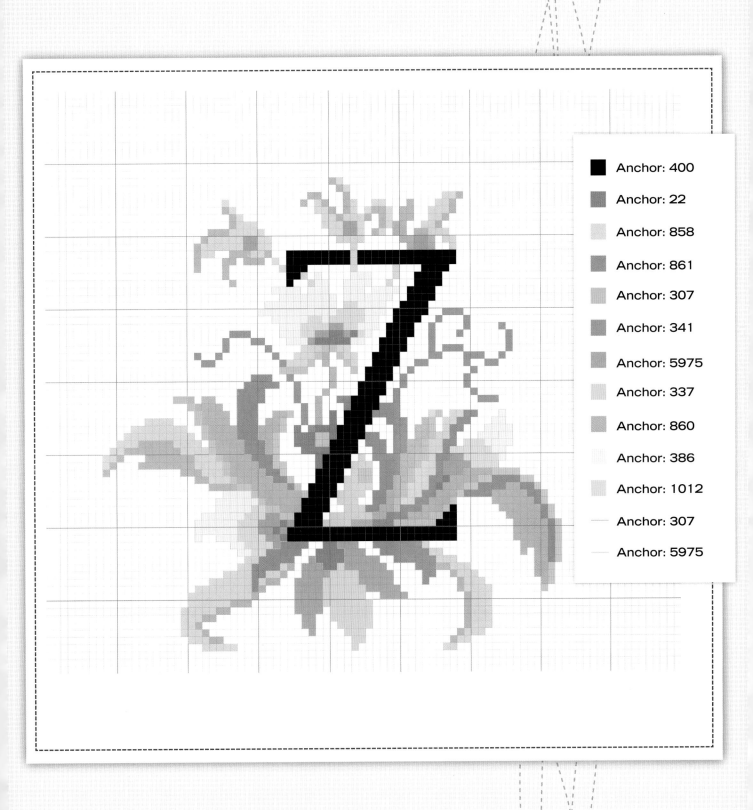

Anchor: 400

Anchor: 22

Anchor: 858

Anchor: 861

Anchor: 307

Anchor: 341

Anchor: 5975

Anchor: 337

Anchor: 860

Anchor: 386

Anchor: 1012

Anchor: 307

Anchor: 5975

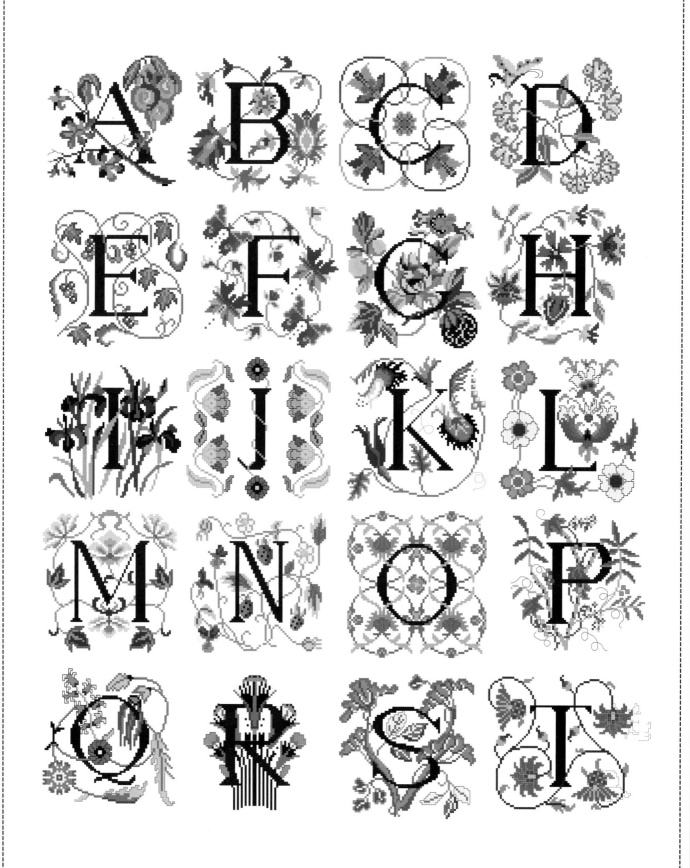

DESIGN ORIGINS

The designs were taken from the following:

A: An eighteenth-century French silk design

B: Persian illuminated letters

C: A sixteenth-century Spanish tile

D: An oriental plate

E: A medieval French mosaic

F: An embroidered falconer's gauntlet from Iran

G: An eighteenth-century French silk design

H: An Indian textile print

I: A seventeenth-century Japanese screen by Korin

J: A Persian prayer rug

K: A fifteenth-century Italian manuscript

L: Islamic architectural borders

M: An oriental vase

N: A fifteenth-century manuscript

O: An Indian manuscript

P: Japanese printed wallpaper

Q: Persian enamelled-ceramic tiles

R: A painted sculptural ornament from ancient Egypt

S: A sixteenth-century Japanese play costume

T: An Indian manuscript border

U: Seventeenth-century Indian cloisonné daggers

V: A Japanese cherry blossom

W: A Chinese stitched carpet

X: Indian textile prints

Y: An Indian sari border

Z: Decorative paintings from Uzbekistan

Working the Appliqué

There are several different ways of working appliqué. The two in this quilt, worked beautifully by Felicity, use outline couching, a method detailed on the following page.

Note that when the bonded fusible web method is used for appliqué, the design pieces will give a mirror image of the original pattern. In this quilt, the two appliqué patches are reverse images, so use pattern 1 to trace the pieces for pattern 2 and vice-versa.

Applique 1
ENLARGE THE IMAGE TO 200%

Applique 2
ENLARGE THE IMAGE TO 200%

A WORD ON NEEDLE SELECTION

A special Appli-bond needle with three sides, which is easier to push through materials such as fusible web, can be found at your local quilting supply store.

Outline Couching

1. On the right side of a cream appliqué piece, use a removable marker to trace as much of pattern 1 as you need for the placement of the pattern pieces and the stems for embroidery.

2. On the paper side of a piece of fusible web, trace the individual pattern pieces for pattern 2, leaving a small gap between each. Cut these out, staying just outside the drawn line. Iron the shapes on the wrong side of the chosen fabrics, then cut them out accurately on the drawn line.

3. Remove the paper from the branch piece. Place the branch, right side up, on the front of the cream fabric and iron it in place. Do the same with each leaf and flower shape. Build up the flower outwards from the center.

4. When the pattern pieces are stuck down, thread two strands of cotton in a needle, tie a small knot in one end, and bring the needle up through the edge of the appliqué piece from the back to the front.

   Unthread the needle. Lay the thread along the edge of the appliqué shape. Thread the needle with one strand of the same color and use this to couch down the original threads with small stitches. Couch by bringing the threaded needle up on the very edge of the appliqué shape, take it over the laid thread and insert the needle almost into the same hole, just catching the edge of the shape.

5. Remove placement marks if necessary, then trim the fabric to 11½" × 6" (29.2 cm × 15.24 cm), making sure the appliqué design is centered.

Outline Couching

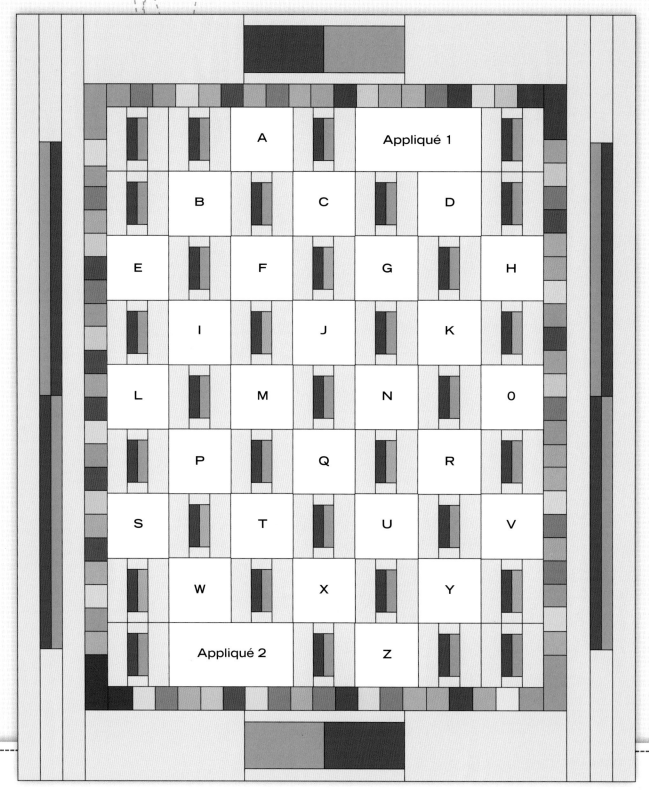

Flowers in Art **Quilt Plan**

Refer to the CD for the letter designs B through Y.

Use ¼" (6 mm) seam allowances throughout. Each finished block measures 5½" × 5½" (14 cm × 14 cm).

Making the Quilt Top

1. Take the thirty-three 1½" × 4½" (3.8 cm × 11.4 cm) red pieces, twenty-six 1½" × 4½" (3.8 cm × 11.4 cm) gold pieces and seven 1½" × 4½" (3.8 cm × 11.4 cm) green pieces. Stitch each red piece to either a gold or green piece down the long side and press open. (Figure A)

2. Add a 1¼" × 2½" (3.2 cm × 6.4 cm) cream piece to each end of the red units and press the seam allowances toward the darker color. (Figure B)

3. Stitch a 2¼" × 6" (5.7 cm × 15.2) cream piece at each side. (Figure C) You now have thirty-three 6" (15.2 cm) blocks.

4. Following the quilt plan, lay out the blocks, stitched letters and appliqué patches. Pin and stitch across in rows. Press the seams away from the embroidered blocks. Stitch the rows together, being careful to match the seam lines. Press seams upward toward the top row.

The quilt center should now measure 39" × 50" (99. 6 cm × 127 cm), including seam allowances.

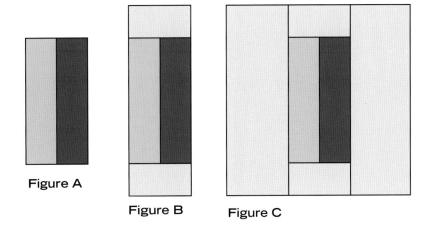

Figure A

Figure B   **Figure C**

Making the Blocks

Adding the Borders and Finishing the Quilt

1. Take the seventy-eight 2½" (6.4 cm) squares and arrange them in two rows of 17 and two rows of 22. Don't stitch them at this point.

2. Place a 2½" × 2¾" (6.3 cm × 7 cm) red at one end of each 17 row and a 2½" × 2¾" (6.3 cm × 7 cm) gold at the other end.

3. Place a 2½" × 5¼" (6.3 cm × 13.33 cm) red at one end of each 22 row and a 2½" × 5¼" (6.3 cm × 13.33 cm) gold at the other end.

4. Check that these red and gold ends will stitch together to form red corners and gold corners at opposite corners of the quilt. Refer to the quilt plan.

    Pin and stitch the short rows, then stitch the rows to the top and bottom of the quilt top. Press open.

    Pin and stitch the long rows and stitch the completed rows to the two sides of the quilt top.

5. Stitch the 1½" × 21" (3.8 cm × 53.3 cm) reds and golds together lengthwise to create four strips-sets, each with one red and one gold strip. Stitch two strip-sets together end to end, alternating the colors. Repeat with the other two strips.

6. Stitch a 2½" × 12¾" (6.3 cm × 32.4 cm) cream piece at each end of both strips.

7. Add a 2½" × 66" (6.43 cm × 167.6 cm) cream strip to each side of the quilt. These are the side borders. Set aside.

8. Stitch together the ends of two 3½" × 7½" (8.9 cm × 19 cm) red and gold pieces to form the center of the top and bottom borders.

9. Add a 3½" × 14¾" (8.9 cm × 37.5 cm) cream piece at each end.

10. Stitch a 2" × 43" (5.1 cm × 109 cm) cream strip lengthwise to each side to complete the top borders. Repeat for the bottom border.

11. Pin and stitch the top and bottom borders to the quilt top. Stitch the side borders in place. Trim the ends even with the sides of the quilt.

12. Make up the quilt sandwich and quilt. Add the binding.

STARRY FLOWERS

This quilt originated from nine tapestry cushion designs I worked in wool. We were getting ready to move to a new house, and each cushion illustrated one of my favorite flowers from the garden I was about to leave behind. Using this series of designs to make a quilt resulted in the perfect keepsake to hang on my wall, reminding me of my time in the garden.

The designs for the cushions were worked on 12-count canvas in tent stitch and cross-stitch using Anchor Tapisserie wool (the colors are indicated by the parenthetical numbers in the color keys), they converted nicely into simple cross-stitch using embroidery floss on 14-count Adia. I chose to work the stitching on black, which makes the completed wall hanging very dramatic. However, the designs could just as well be stitched on cream, off-white or, indeed, any other color if you are daunted by the idea of using black.

Only seven of the nine original designs were incorporated into this project, but the charts for the other two—gladioli and geranium—are on the disk, shown as cushions. Feel free to choose which of the nine flowers you'd like to include in your quilt.

Making the Flying Geese Unit

To make a Flying Goose pattern, draw a diagonal line from corner to corner on the wrong side of two black 2¾" (7 cm) squares. (Figure A) Place one square on one of the 2¾" × 5" (7 cm × 12.7 cm) rectangles right sides facing, matching two corners. Sew along the drawn line. Trim the seam to ¼" (6 mm) (figure B) and press the triangle towards the corner. Repeat with the second black square on the opposite two corners (figure C), so the drawn lines make a V, forming a colored triangle with black corners. (Figure D)

Materials

FOR THE STITCHERY

Seven 12" (30.5 cm) square of black 14-count Aida or 28-count evenweave

1 skein of embroidery floss in each of the colors listed on the color key for each flower

FOR THE PATCHWORK

1 yd. (0.9 m) light green, cut the following:

thirty-two 2¾" (7 cm) squares

ten 2¾" × 5" (7 cm × 12.7 cm) pieces

four 2¾" × 11¾" (7 cm × 29.8 cm) strips

six 2¾" × 13½" (7 cm × 34.3) strips

½ yd. (45.7 cm) dark green cut thirty-two 2¾" (7 cm) squares

½ yd. (45.7 cm) black cut seventy-six 2¾" (7 cm) black squares

Four 2¾" × 5" (7 cm × 12.7 cm) fabric pieces of each color to match the flower squares

Small amounts of fabric in colors to match the flowers

Backing and batting, 30¾" × 48¼" (78.1 cm × 122.6 cm)

Binding, ¼ yd. (22.9 cm) for approximately 1½" × 160" (3.8 cm × 406 cm)

Figure A

Figure B

Figure C

Figure D

Starry Flowers
Finished size: 30¾" × 48¼" (78.1 cm × 122.6 cm)

Working the Embroidery

1. First, overcast the edges to prevent them from fraying. Work the designs in cross-stitch in the center of the fabric.

2. Spray the wrong side of the flower blocks with starch before pressing with a dry iron. Trim the blocks to 9½" × 9½" (24 cm × 24 cm), making sure the stitching is centered.

Flower 1: Nasturtiums

Anchor: 19		
Anchor: 45	Anchor: 293	
Anchor: 214 ○	● Anchor: 298	
Anchor: 215	+ Anchor: 330	
Anchor: 217	— Anchor: 332	
Anchor: 254 ⊖	Anchor: 334	

Flower 2: Fuchsia

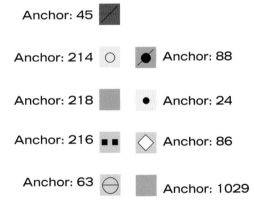

Anchor: 45

Anchor: 214 ○   ◑ Anchor: 88

Anchor: 218   ● Anchor: 24

Anchor: 216 ■■   ◇ Anchor: 86

Anchor: 63 ⊖   Anchor: 1029

Flower 3: Scabious

Anchor: 02 ○   Anchor: 256

Anchor: 92 ▦   ▽ Anchor: 899

Anchor: 108 ╱ | Anchor: 264

Anchor: 109 ●   ◇ Anchor: 268

Flower 4: Icelandic Poppies

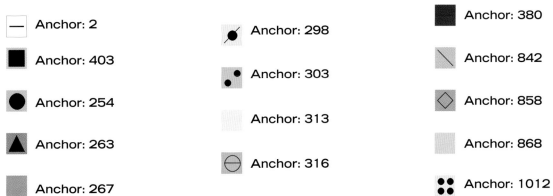

— Anchor: 2	Anchor: 298	Anchor: 380
Anchor: 403	Anchor: 303	Anchor: 842
Anchor: 254	Anchor: 313	Anchor: 858
Anchor: 263	Anchor: 316	Anchor: 868
Anchor: 267		Anchor: 1012

Flower 5: Clematis

Anchor: 108   ▬ Anchor: 268

Anchor: 118 ▲   ∩ Anchor: 275

Anchor: 264 ○   Anchor: 340 / 266

Anchor: 266 ✕   ⊡ Anchor: 883

Anchor: 267   ╱ Anchor: 4220

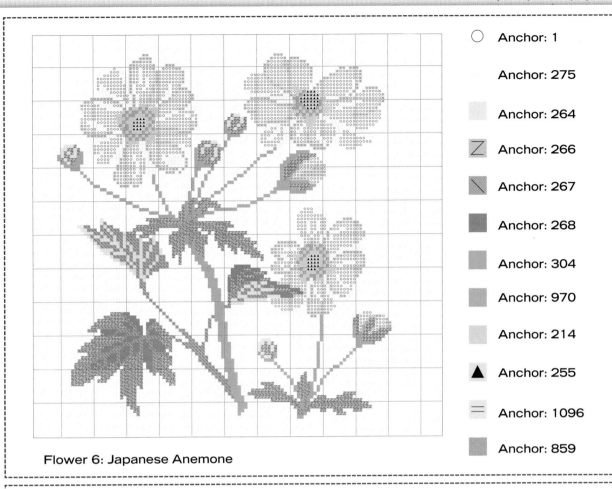

○	Anchor: 1
	Anchor: 275
	Anchor: 264
⧄	Anchor: 266
⧅	Anchor: 267
	Anchor: 268
	Anchor: 304
	Anchor: 970
	Anchor: 214
▲	Anchor: 255
=	Anchor: 1096
	Anchor: 859

Flower 6: Japanese Anemone

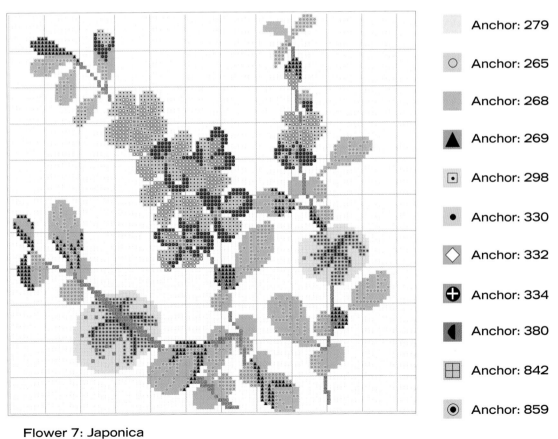

	Anchor: 279
○	Anchor: 265
	Anchor: 268
▲	Anchor: 269
⊡	Anchor: 298
•	Anchor: 330
◇	Anchor: 332
⊕	Anchor: 334
◖	Anchor: 380
⊞	Anchor: 842
⊙	Anchor: 859

Flower 7: Japonica

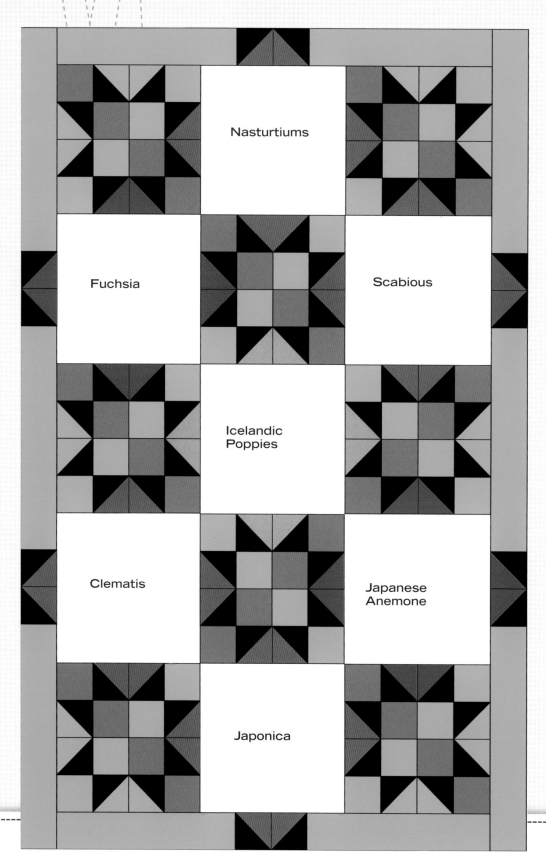

Nasturtiums

Fuchsia

Scabious

Icelandic
Poppies

Clematis

Japanese
Anemone

Japonica

Starry Flowers Quilt Plan

Use ¼" (6 mm) seam allowances throughout. Each finished block measures 9½" × 9½" (24.1 cm × 24.1 cm).

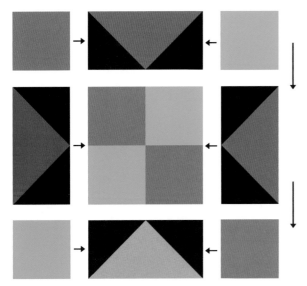

Assembling an Evening Star Block

Completed Evening Star Block

Making the Evening Star Blocks

1. Referring to page 97, make the 2¾" (7 cm) black squares and the 2¾" × 5" (7 cm × 12.7 cm) rectangles into Flying Geese blocks. You will have 28 geese units with colored blocks and 10 with green blocks.

2. For the four-patch centers, stitch one light green and one dark green square together. Press the seam to the dark side. Repeat this. Now join the two sets together to make a four-patch. The seams should now face opposite ways and fit neatly together. Make 8 of these units.

3. Matching the colored geese units to the quilt plan (or your own plan if you have altered the design), arrange two light green and two dark green squares, one four-patch unit, and four geese units, making sure the geese units point into the center and the four-patch has a dark green square at the top left and bottom right.

4. Stitch a dark green square to the left of the top geese unit and a light green square to the right. Press the seams to the right.

5. Stitch the geese units vertically to the right and left of the four-patch. Press the seams to the left.

6. Stitch the light green square to the left of the bottom geese unit and the dark green to the right. Press the seams to the right.

7. Pin and stitch the rows together. Press the seams outward. You have now completed one Evening Star block. Repeat to make 7 more blocks.

Making the Quilt Top

1. Arrange the flower blocks and pieced blocks, taking care with the position of the colored geese.

2. Pin and stitch the top row. Press seams toward the flower square.

3. Do the same with the other rows, then pin and stitch the rows together. The seams should fit neatly together. Press once more before moving on.

Adding the Borders and Finishing the Quilt

1. Take the geese unit that needs to fit in the top border. Stitch one 2¾" × 11¾" (7 cm × 29.8 cm) green border strip at each edge of the unit. Pin and stitch this to the top of the quilt. Do the same for the bottom. Press open.

2. Keeping the geese in the right order for your quilt, pin and stitch one 2¾" × 13½" (7 cm × 34.3 cm) green border strip between the two geese for the left border and one at each end, making sure the geese units point outward. Pin and stitch this border in place. Do the same for the right edge. Press open.

3. Make the quilt sandwich of the backing, batting and top. Quilt in the ditch around the flower squares, then add any other quilting that you wish on the Evening Star blocks and borders. Bind the edges as usual.

4. If you choose, add small wooden buttons to the center of the four-patch units.

HISTORICAL BLACKWORK ANIMALS

After spending considerable time researching designs in the Victoria and Albert Museum in London, I kept returning to ceramic tile designs by William De Morgan—a contemporary of William Morris and Edward Burne-Jones—imagining these designs in blackwork.

De Morgan produced numerous designs based on plants and animals. The inspiration for the embroidery in this project was taken from four designs: a fantastical bird, an antelope, a fish and a dodo.

The blackwork stitching uses two shades of gray, which is not as harsh as black (perhaps it should be called "graywork"), and the color of the patchwork cottons follows the gray theme with a red relief. Changing out the red for another color would yield an equally dramatic quilt, so if you're aiming to match the décor in a specific room, don't be afraid to use a different color.

THE HISTORY OF BLACKWORK

Blackwork embroidery is basically a form of counted-thread work where patterns are formed by straight stitches in black or red (called *scarletwork*) on a contrasting evenly-woven background. Originally, the technique was associated with dress, especially on sleeves and chemises. It is thought to have been brought from Spain to England in 1501 by Catharine of Aragon at the time of her marriage to Henry VIII. Its popularity continued through the sixteenth century, but declined somewhat after that. It had a revival during the 1930s, when many original patterns were used for decoration.

Today, the term *blackwork* refers to the technique rather than the color used. It is used more freely and is recognized as a creative art form.

In this design, shaded blackwork is achieved by varying the color, the thickness of thread and the density of the stitches.

Historical Blackwork Animals
Finished size of quilt 31" × 47" (78.7 cm × 119.4 cm)

Materials

FOR THE STITCHERY

Four 8" (20.3 cm) squares of 14-count Aida or 28-count evenweave (work over 2 threads)

1 skein each of Anchor embroidery floss in 235 and 236

FOR THE PATCHWORK

⅝ yd. (57.2 cm) assorted grays; cut as follows:

  fifteen 1½" (3.8 cm) squares for the nine patches (dark gray centers)

  one-hundred and twenty 1½" (3.8 cm) squares (mixed grays)

  eight 4½" (10.8 cm) squares for the center surrounds (mixed grays)

  two 1½" × 24½" (3.8 cm × 62.2 cm) for the top and bottom borders

  twenty-six 2½" × 3½" (6.4 cm × 8.9 cm) for the side borders

¼ yd. (23 cm) special gray, cut the following:

  two 1½" × 25½" (3.8 cm × 64.7 cm) strips

  four 2½" × 3½" (6.4 cm × 8.9 cm) pieces for each end of the pieced border.

⅛ yd. (11.4 cm) of a contrasting fabric to cut four 3½" (8.9 cm) squares (Japanese fabric used here)

¾ yd. (69 cm) black; cut the following:

  two 2½" × 31" (6.4 cm × 78.7 cm) border strips

  two 2½" × 43½" (6.4 cm × 110.5 cm) border strips.

  twenty-two 4" (10.2 cm) squares

⅝ yd. (57.2 cm) red; cut the following:

  two 1½" × 42" (3.8 cm × 106.7 cm) border strips (If the fabric width is shorter than 42" [106.7 cm], join two strips to get the required length.)

  two 1½" × 27" (3.8 cm × 68.6 cm) border strips.

  twenty-two 4" (10.2 cm) squares.

Backing and batting, 36" × 52" (91.4 cm × 132 cm)

Binding, ¼ yd. (22.9 cm) for 1½" × 156" (3.8 cm × 397 cm)

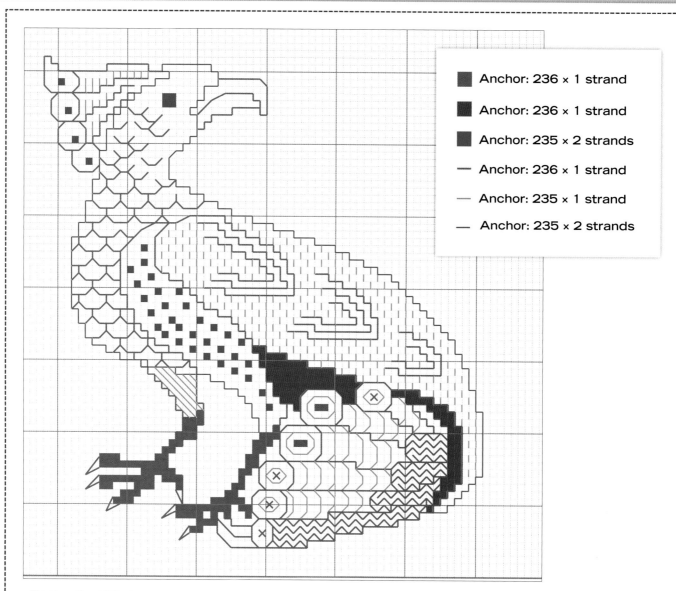

■	Anchor: 236 × 1 strand
■	Anchor: 236 × 1 strand
■	Anchor: 235 × 2 strands
—	Anchor: 236 × 1 strand
—	Anchor: 235 × 1 strand
—	Anchor: 235 × 2 strands

Fantastical Bird

Working the Embroidery

1. Using one strand or two as directed by the key, work the designs. Work the lines in backstitch, single running or seeding stitches. In those areas where the whole square is colored, work a cross-stitch again following the color key for the color and number of strands. Try not to carry threads across large areas at the back, especially across spaces, as they may be visible when the stitched piece is incorporated into the whole project. It is better to finish the thread off by threading it under a few stitches at the back. You can start a new thread in the same way.

2. When the four designs have been stitched, lightly spray the back of the fabric with starch and press on the wrong side with a moderate iron on top of an ironing blanket or folded towel. Using starch will help to make the fabric easier to handle while cutting and stitching, and reduce fraying. Then, center the design and cut out a 6½" (16.5 cm) square. This is now ready to be incorporated into the patchwork.

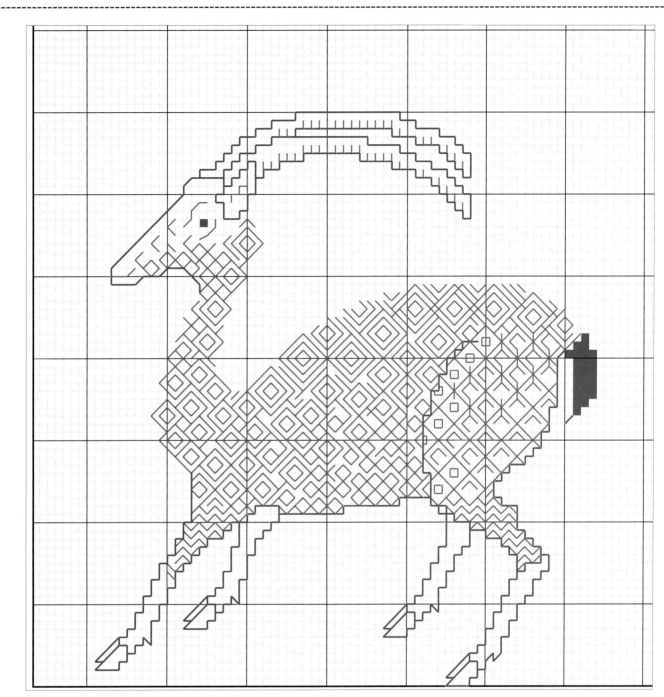

Antelope

■ Anchor: 235 × 2 strands

— Anchor: 236 × 1 strand

— Anchor: 235 × 2 strands

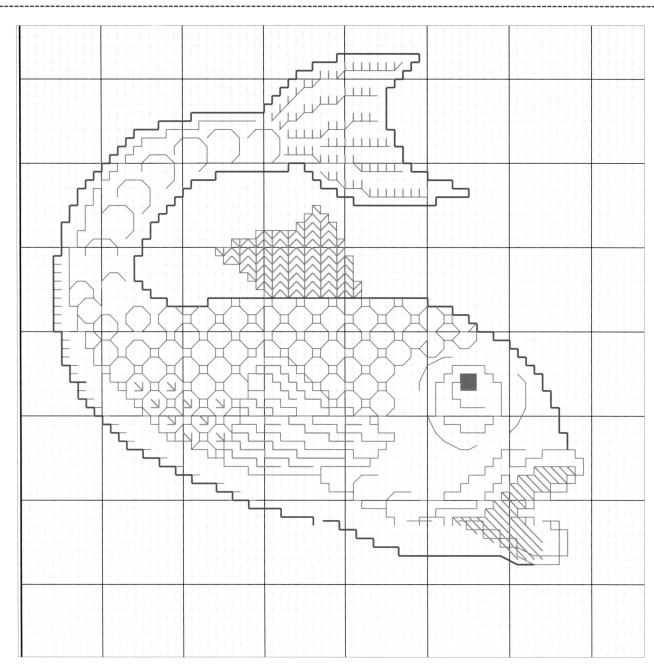

Fish

■ Anchor: 236 × 1 strand

— Anchor: 236 × 1 strand

— Anchor: 235 × 1 strand

— Anchor: 235 × 2 strands

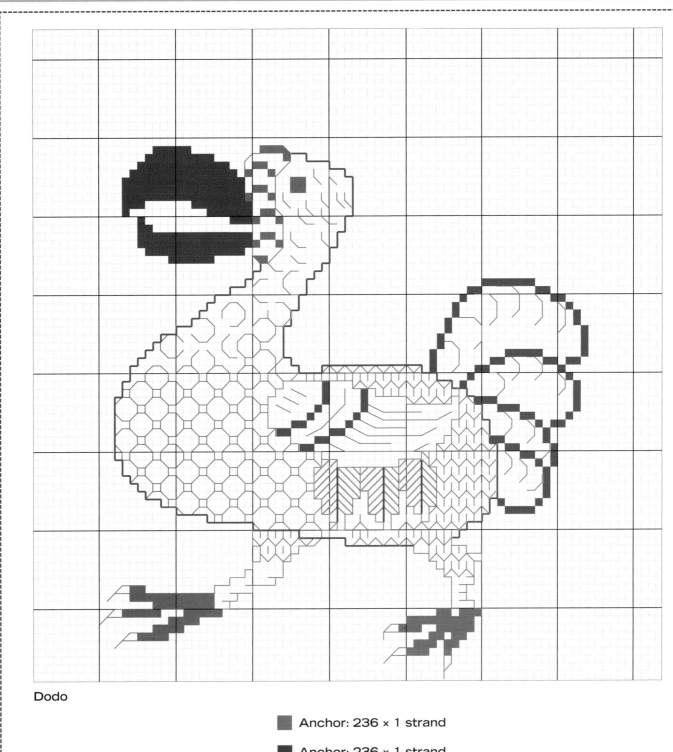

Dodo

■ Anchor: 236 × 1 strand

■ Anchor: 236 × 1 strand

■ Anchor: 235 × 2 strands

— Anchor: 236 × 1 strand

— Anchor: 235 × 1 strand

— Anchor: 236 × 1 strand

— Anchor: 235 × 2 strands

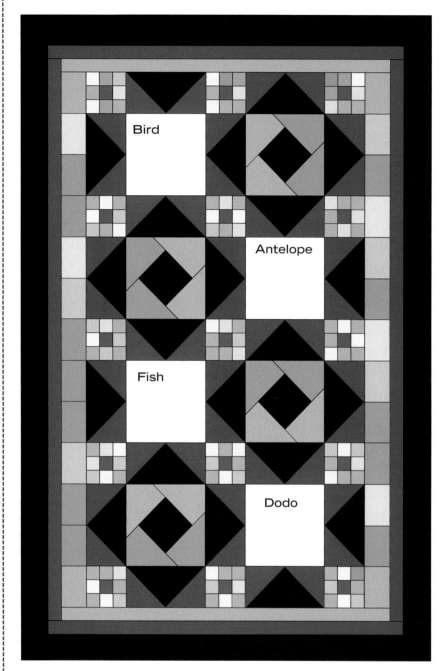

Piecing the Patchwork

1. Join one black and one red square to make two half-square triangle units (see page 32). Repeat with the remaining black and red squares. Trim to 3½" (8.9 cm), cutting off the dog-ears.

   Join these in pairs with the black sides together to form points. These are the Flying Geese red and black units.

2. Arrange eight 1½" (3.8 cm) gray squares randomly around each 1½" (3.8 cm) dark gray center to form nine-patch units, then stitch in rows. Press the seams open.

   Stitch the rows together and trim the completed block to 3½" (8.9 cm).

3. Draw a diagonal line across each of the 4½" (10.8 cm) gray squares and cut to give 16 triangles. Arrange these around each 3½" (8.9 cm) center square, making sure the grays are mixed up.

4. Take one of the center squares and fold to find the center of one side. Mark the center of the long side of one of the triangles. With right sides together, pin one side of the square to the long side of the

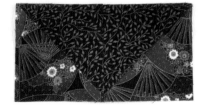

Flying Geese Red and Black Units

Historical Blackwork Animals Quilt Plan

Because this quilt has overlapping blocks that allow the stitching to fill the gaps, it is best assembled by following the instructions.

Use ¼" (6 mm) seam allowances throughout. Each finished block measures 12" × 12" (30.5 cm × 30.5 cm).

triangle, matching the center marks (the triangle edges will extend beyond the square). Working on the back of the square, stitch the two together, starting the stitching 1" (2.5 cm) from the end. Finger-press the seam open.

5. Mark the center of the adjacent side (at the end where the stitching finished) and the center of the long side of the next triangle. Pin, right sides together, and stitch right across from edge to edge (don't start away from the end in this time). Press the seam. Repeat with the third triangle.

6. Fold and pin back the loose corner of the first triangle so that the fourth triangle can be stitched right across without catching it. Press the seam open.

7. Now, pin the loose end over the fourth triangle and stitch, working out from the 1" (2.5 cm) mark. The block should be 6½" (16.5 cm). Repeat for the other three center blocks.

Stitching the triangles to the center square

Making the Quilt Top

1. The easiest way to assemble the quilt is by working in horizontal rows, starting at the top and following the plan.

   Take three nine-patch units and two Flying Geese units. Arrange them as they appear in the diagram to the right, then pin and stitch. Press seams all one direction.

2. Take three Flying Geese units, one 6½" (16.5 cm) center block and the fantastical bird. Arrange them according to the diagram, pin and stitch. Press the seams in the opposite direction to row 1.

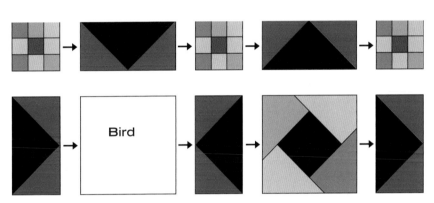

Assembling the Top Two Rows

3. Stitch rows 3, 4, 5, 6, 7, 8 and 9 in the same way, alternating seams between each row. Now stitch the rows together, taking care to match the seams.

Adding the Borders and Finishing the Quilt

1. Randomly arrange the 2½" × 3½" (6.4 cm × 8.9 cm) gray rectangles and sew them, short end together, to form two strips, each with 13 rectangles. Make sure one of the four special gray pieces is at each end of both rows. Press, then pin and stitch one strip to each side of the quilt top, matching seams.

Press the seam allowances toward the border.

2. Pin and stitch a 1½" × 25½" (3.8 cm × 64.7 cm) special gray strip at the top and bottom. Press the seams toward the border.

3. Stitch a 1½" × 42" (3.8 cm × 106.7 cm) red border strip at each side and press open. Then a 27" × 1½" (3.8 cm × 68.6 cm) red border strip at the top and bottom.

4. Stitch a 2½" × 43½" (6.4 cm × 110.6 cm) black border strip to each side and press open. Then a 2½" × 31" (6.4 cm × 78.7 cm) black border strip at the top and bottom.

5. Make the quilt sandwich, then quilt. Add a 1½" (3.8 cm) wide binding strip to complete.

114

SASHIKO CHARM

Sashiko is an ancient Japanese method of stitching several layers of fabric together, using a simple running stitch to secure them. This made garments warmer, stronger and more durable. Even after fabrics became cheaper and more readily available, the same technique was widely used for bedcovers, curtains and other household items.

Today, a running stitch is still used to create simple repetitive designs or interlocking patterns in which the spaces between the lines of stitching are as important as the stitching itself. Traditional Japanese designs, many taken from nature or from family crests with symbolic elements, are incorporated into sashiko stitching as decorative features. The designs stitched in this project include hemp leaves, grasses, scale weights and a variation of the Seven Treasures design.

Traditionally, indigo-dyed cottons in a variety of wonderful blues were used for sashiko, with stitching in cream or white. I used this color scheme for the borders of my wall hanging, but I substituted pinstriped navy suiting material for the cotton. If you prefer to use washable fabric, any firm or tightly woven dark blue cotton would be suitable. For the decorative circles and diamonds, I used a charm pack with Japanese prints. Though 100 percent cotton thread especially made for sashiko work is available, the size 8 cream Perlé cotton I used for this project produced good results. Four strands of standard embroidery cotton also would work.

Materials

FOR THE STITCHERY

2 balls Perlé 8 creme cotton

1 ball Perlé 8 in terracotta

12 buttons for the centers of the diamonds

4 buttons for the corners

FOR THE PATCHWORK

½ yd. (45.7 cm) cream fabric for nineteen 5" (12.7 cm) background squares

Six 5" (12.5 cm) terracotta squares for background squares

Forty-one 5" (12.5 cm) squares of assorted colors (28 blue, 8 cream and 5 terracotta) for the circles and diamonds

¾ yd. (69 cm) blue fabric; cut the following:

two 6" × 34" (15.2 cm × 86.4 cm) strips for the border

two 6" × 26" (15.2 cm × 66 cm) strips for the border

Backing and batting, 35" × 35" (89 cm × 89 cm)

Binding, ¼ yd. (22.9 cm) either navy or terracotta for approximately 1½" × 121" (3.8 cm × 307 cm)

Thin card for templates

Sashiko Charm
Finished size: 30" × 30" (76 cm × 76 cm)

Finished Hemp Leaf Border

Finished Scale Weights Border

Finished Seven Treasures Border

Finished Grasses Border

The Sashiko Borders

Adding these stitched patterns to the border requires you to draw a grid on the fabric using a quilter's pencil or pen, or a soapstone marker. Check that the marker you choose can be removed either with a brush or water. Look carefully at the manufacturer's instructions about removal to make sure it is compatible with your chosen fabric.

The patterns provided on the next few pages assume you will be drawing on the front of your fabric. However, as the borders of this hanging are embroidered before the quilt is made up, you could draw the grid on the back of the fabric so you don't have to worry about removing any unsightly marks. In this case, you would work the stitching from the back, so the patterns would be reversed.

Stitching the Sashiko

1. Sashiko uses a simple running stitch. It is important that the stitches are the same size and should be longer on the right side as they form the pattern. A long needle enables several running stitches to be done at the same time, which helps to keep the stitching lines straighter. Note that the stitched borders on the photographed quilt may be slightly longer than the original patterns indicate. To make it easier for you to draw, the measurements are given here in ¼" (6 mm). If you would like it to be longer, just continue the pattern.

2. Start with a small knot and finish by threading under the stitches.

3. When patterns cross, make the stitches cross on the wrong side. Where there is a point, make one of the stitches go into the point to define it. When turning a corner or point, keep the thread slack rather than pulling it tight to avoid puckering.

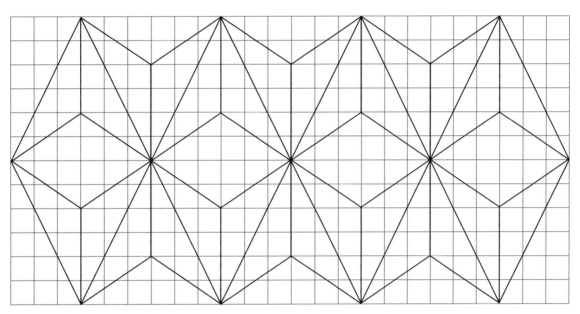

Hemp Leaf Pattern

one square = ¼" [6 mm]

Hemp Leaf (Bottom Border)

1. Using a quilter's ruler, draw a 3" × 19½" (7.6 cm × 49.5 cm) box in the center of the wrong side of one of the short border strips. Fill this box with a ¼" (6 mm) grid of 12 × 78 squares. Keep the marker point sharp so the line is clear and doesn't become thick, as this distorts the measurement. Don't panic if the box has to be extended slightly—there is some leeway for error!

2. Copy the pattern onto the grid, starting at the left side and working across.

3. Stitch the pattern. Outline the box using the Perlé cotton 386.

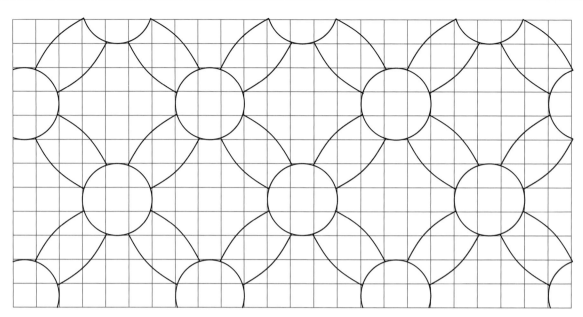

Seven Treasures Pattern

one square = ¼" [6 mm]

Seven Treasures Variation (Top Border)

1. Draw a 3" × 19¾" (7.6 cm × 50 cm) box on a short border strip and fill this with a ¼" (6 mm) grid to give 12 × 79 squares. Either use a coin measuring ¾" (1.9 cm) or make a card template of the small ¾" (1.9 cm) circle and use this to draw the circles.

2. Draw the curved lines to connect them using a 2" (5.1 cm) circle template.

3. Stitch the pattern, then outline the box as for the Hemp Leaf pattern (page 117).

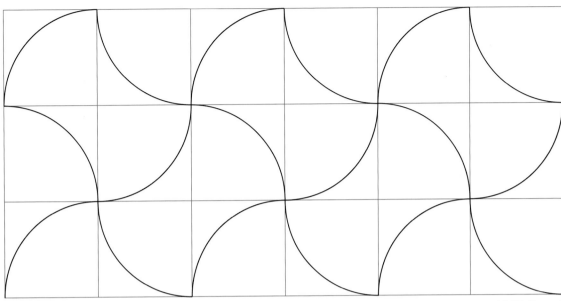

Scale Weights Pattern

one square = 1" [2.5 cm]

Scale Weights (Left Side Border)

1. Draw a 3" × 24" (7.6 cm × 61 cm) box and fill this with a 1" (2.5 cm) grid of 3 × 24 squares. Make a template of the curved shape, then draw around this on each square.

2. Stitch the pattern, then outline the box as for the Hemp Leaf pattern (page 117).

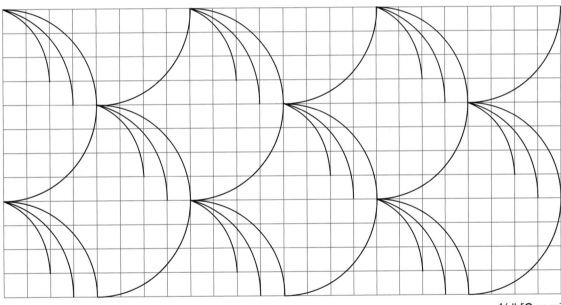

Grasses Pattern

one square = ¼" [6 mm]

Grasses (Right Side Border)

1. Draw a 3" × 24" (7.6 cm × 61 cm) box and fill this with a ¼" (6 mm) grid of 12 × 96 squares. Use a 2" (5.1 cm) circle template to draw the curves, or draw them freehand.

2. Stitch the pattern, then outline the box as for the Hemp Leaf pattern (page 117).

Sashiko Charm Quilt Plan

Use ¼" (6 mm) seam allowances throughout Each finished block measures 4½" × 4½" (11.4 cm × 11.4 cm).

Making the Quilt Blocks

1. Arrange the cream and terracotta background squares to form the pattern according to the Plan for the Center.

2. For each diamond, cut four matching 2" (5.1 cm) squares. Use one of the blue 5" (12.5 cm) squares for each diamond.

3. Following the Plan for the Corners, lay these squares on the corners of the background squares so that (a) squares have one corner, the (b) squares have two corners, the (c) squares have three corners, and the center (d) square has no corners.

4. Take the top left background square. This has only one small square laid on it. On the back of the small square, draw a diagonal line through the corners. Pin the small square on top of the background square, right sides together, so that the line runs off the edges, not toward the center. Stitch along the drawn line. Trim the seam to ¼" (6 mm) and press. You now have a cream square with a blue corner. Stitch the corners to each background square, then trim each of these units to 5" (12.7 cm).

5. Pin and stitch together the five units in the top row, matching the diamond points carefully. Press the seams to the right. Do the same with the second row, pressing the seams to the left. Continue with the other rows, alternating seams between rows. Then pin and stitch the rows together, pressing the seams toward the bottom.

Plan for the Center

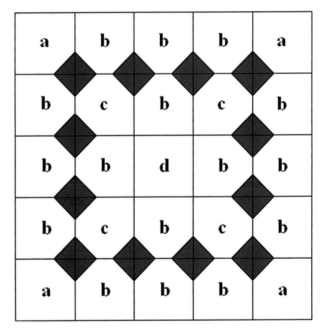

Plan for the Corners

Preparing the Circles

1. Make a thin card template for the larger (3" [7.6 cm]) circle by tracing it on paper, then sticking the paper to a piece of cardstock and carefully cutting it out.

2. Draw around the template on the back of twenty-five of the 5" (12.5 cm) squares, then cut out each one, adding a ¼" (6 mm) allowance all the way round.

← 3" (7.6 cm) →

Secure Template

Place a fabric circle wrong side up on the ironing board. Center the circle template on top of the fabric. Pin to secure.

Iron Fabric

Press the seam allowance on top of the card circle.

Baste the Seam Allowance

Remove the card and gently press the right side of the fabric circle, then baste the seam allowance in place.

Prepared Circles

Your circle is now ready to be appliquéd to the center of one of the squares on the quilt top. Repeat with the other circles.

Making the Quilt Top

1. Arrange the larger circles on the square units of the quilt top as show in the Plan for the Circles, then stitch in place. Snip the basting thread with a pair of scissors and pull the thread out of the fabric circles.

2. Repeat this procedure with the smaller (2½" [6.4 cm]) circles around the center squares as shown in the Plan for the Smaller Circles.

   The quilt top should measure 22½" × 22½" (57 cm × 57 cm).

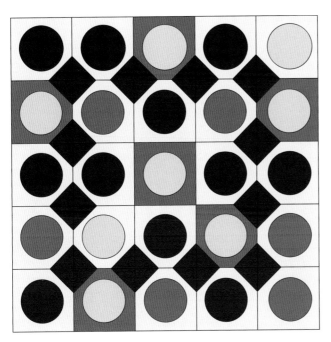

Plan for the Circles

Plan for Adding the Smaller Circles

Adding the Borders and Finishing the Quilt

1. Centering the terracotta box along the border strips, trim the short border strips to 4½" × 22½" (11.4 cm × 57 cm) then pin and stitch them in place to the top and bottom edges of the quilt and press open.

2. Again, keeping the pattern in the center, trim the long border strips to 4½" × 30½" (11.4 cm × 77.5 cm). Pin and stitch these to the sides of the quilt and press open.

3. To scallop the corners, draw around one quarter of a 4" (10.2 cm) circle, placing the center of the circle on the corner of the quilt. Trim the edge, allowing for a ¼" (6 mm) seam allowance.

4. Make the quilt sandwich. Quilt in the ditch around the squares, diamonds and edge of the circles. Bind using either navy or terracotta.

5. Add buttons to the centers of the diamonds or tie with one of the Perlé cottons, then add a button to each corner.

Adding the Borders

ANCHOR TO DMC CONVERSION CHART

Anchor brand embroidery floss is my favorite to use, but it may not be readily available in shops in your area. DMC is an equally wonderful brand and it is easy to find. The chart below will help you find the color matches for the embroidery floss used in this book. These charts can also be found most places embroidery floss is sold.

001 > 5200	088 > 917	175 > 794	266 > 471	351 > 400	851 > 924	936 > 632	1041 > 844
002 > White	089 > 718	176 > 793	267 > 469	352 > 300	852 > 3047	939 > 3755	1042 > 504
006 > 353	090 > 3836	177 > 792	268 > 937	355 > 975	853 > 372	940 > 824	1043 > 369
008 > 3824	092 > 553	178 > 791	269 > 936	357 > 433	854 > 371	941 > 792	1044 > 895
009 > 352	094 > 917	185 > 964	271 > 819	358 > 433	855 > 370	942 > 738	1045 > 436
010 > 351	095 > 3609	186 > 959	273 > 645	359 > 801	856 > 370	943 > 422	1046 > 435
011 > 350	096 > 3608	187 > 958	274 > 928	360 > 898	858 > 524	944 > 869	1047 > 402
013 > 817	097 > 554	188 > 3812	275 > 746	361 > 738	859 > 523	945 > 834	1048 > 3776
019 > 304	098 > 553	189 > 991	276 > 543	362 > 437	860 > 522	956 > 613	1049 > 301
020 > 816	099 > 552	203 > 954	277 > 830	363 > 977	861 > 935	968 > 778	1050 > 3781
022 > 815	100 > 327	204 > 913	278 > 3819	365 > 435	862 > 520	969 > 223	1060 > 3811
023 > 963	101 > 550	205 > 911	279 > 734	366 > 951	868 > 3779	970 > 3687	1062 > 598
024 > 776	102 > 550	206 > 564	280 > 733	367 > 738	869 > 3743	972 > 3803	1064 > 597
025 > 3716	103 > 211	208 > 563	281 > 732	368 > 437	870 > 3042	975 > 828	1066 > 3809
026 > 894	108 > 210	209 > 912	288 > 445	369 > 402	871 > 3041	976 > 3752	1068 > 3808
027 > 893	109 > 209	210 > 562	289 > 307	370 > 434	872 > 3740	977 > 334	1070 > 993
028 > 956	110 > 208	211 > 918	290 > 444	371 > 975	873 > 3740	978 > 322	1072 > 992
029 > 891	111 > 208	212 > 561	291 > 444	372 > 738	874 > 834	979 > 312	1074 > 3814
031 > 3708	112 > 3837	213 > 504	292 > 3078	373 > 3828	875 > 3817	1001 > 976	1076 > 991
033 > 3706	117 > 341	214 > 368	293 > 727	374 > 420	876 > 3816	1002 > 977	1080 > 842
035 > 3705	118 > 340	215 > 320	295 > 726	375 > 869	877 > 3815	1003 > 922	1082 > 841
036 > 3326	119 > 3840	216 > 562	297 > 973	376 > 3776	878 > 501	1004 > 920	1084 > 840
038 > 956	120 > 3747	217 > 367	298 > 972	378 > 841	879 > 500	1005 > 816	1086 > 839
039 > 309	121 > 794	218 > 319	300 > 745	379 > 840	880 > 951	1006 > 304	1088 > 838
040 > 956	122 > 3807	225 > 702	301 > 744	380 > 838	881 > 945	1007 > 3772	1089 > 3843
041 > 893	123 > 791	226 > 702	302 > 743	381 > 938	882 > 758	1008 > 3773	1090 > 996
042 > 309	127 > 823	227 > 701	303 > 742	382 > 3371	883 > 3064	1009 > 3770	1092 > 964
043 > 815	128 > 3756	228 > 700	304 > 741	386 > 3823	884 > 920	1010 > 951	1094 > 605
044 > 815	129 > 3325	229 > 910	305 > 725	387 > Ecru	885 > 739	1011 > 948	1096 > 3753
045 > 814	130 > 799	230 > 909	306 > 3820	388 > 842	886 > 677	1012 > 754	1098 > 3801
046 > 666	131 > 798	231 > 453	307 > 783	390 > 822	887 > 3046	1013 > 3778	1200 > 62
047 > 321	132 > 797	232 > 452	308 > 782	391 > 3033	888 > 3045	1014 > 355	1201 > 48
048 > 818	133 > 796	233 > 451	309 > 781	392 > 642	889 > 610	1015 > 3777	1202 > 112
049 > 3689	134 > 820	234 > 762	310 > 434	393 > 3790	890 > 729	1016 > 3727	1203 > 57
050 > 957	136 > 799	235 > 414	311 > 3827	397 > 3024	891 > 676	1017 > 316	1204 > 107
052 > 899	137 > 798	236 > 3799	313 > 977	398 > 415	892 > 225	1018 > 3726	1206 > 115
054 > 956	139 > 797	238 > 703	314 > 741	399 > 318	893 > 224	1019 > 315	1207 > 99
055 > 604	140 > 3755	239 > 702	316 > 971	400 > 317	894 > 224	1020 > 3713	1208 > 95
057 > 601	142 > 798	240 > 966	323 > 722	401 > 413	895 > 223	1021 > 761	1209 > 126
059 > 3350	143 > 797	241 > 989	324 > 721	403 > 310	896 > 3721	1022 > 760	1210 > 121
060 > 3688	144 > 800	242 > 989	326 > 720	410 > 995	897 > 221	1023 > 3712	1211 > 93
062 > 603	145 > 799	243 > 988	328 > 3341	433 > 996	898 > 611	1024 > 3328	1212 > 67
063 > 602	146 > 798	244 > 987	329 > 3340	681 > 3051	899 > 3782	1025 > 347	1213 > 101
065 > 3350	147 > 797	245 > 987	330 > 947	683 > 500	900 > 648	1026 > 225	1214 > 125
066 > 3688	148 > 311	246 > 986	332 > 946	778 > 3774	901 > 680	1027 > 3722	1215 > 114
068 > 3687	149 > 336	253 > 472	333 > 900	779 > 3768	903 > 3032	1028 > 3685	1216 > 94
069 > 3803	150 > 336	254 > 472	334 > 606	830 > 644	905 > 3021	1029 > 915	1217 > 104
070 > 3685	152 > 939	255 > 907	335 > 606	831 > 613	906 > 829	1030 > 3746	1218 > 105
072 > 3865	158 > 747	256 > 906	336 > 3341	832 > 612	907 > 832	1031 > 3753	1219 > 108
073 > 963	159 > 827	257 > 905	337 > 3778	842 > 3013	914 > 407	1032 > 3752	1220 > 51
074 > 605	160 > 827	258 > 904	338 > 3778	843 > 3012	920 > 932	1033 > 932	1223 > 53
075 > 3733	161 > 813	259 > 772	339 > 920	844 > 3012	921 > 931	1034 > 931	1243 > 111
076 > 3687	162 > 517	260 > 3364	340 > 919	845 > 730	922 > 930	1035 > 930	4146 > 950
077 > 3687	164 > 824	261 > 3053	341 > 918	846 > 3011	923 > 699	1036 > 3750	5975 > 3830
078 > 917	167 > 598	262 > 3052	342 > 211	847 > 3072	924 > 731	1037 > 3756	8581 > 3022
085 > 3609	168 > 807	263 > 3362	343 > 3752	848 > 927	926 > 712	1038 > 519	9046 > 321
086 > 3608	169 > 806	264 > 3348	347 > 3064	849 > 927	928 > 3761	1039 > 518	9159 > 828
087 > 3607	170 > 3765	265 > 3348	349 > 301	850 > 926	933 > 543	1040 > 647	9575 > 758

Patchwork & Stitchery
12 Quilt Projects with Embroidered Twists
By Carol Phillipson

For further information, contact:

Krause Publications
4700 East Galbraith Road
Cincinnati, OH 45236

Embroidery Design Copyright Information

Printing from CD:

Embroidery charts and piecing and embroidery templates on this CD have been presented in JPEG, BITMAP (.bmp) and PDF format. Your computer system likely has built-in software to open these files. To use your default software, simply double-click on desired template.

To use JPEG images, you will require software that allows you to import JPEGs. This includes Adobe Creative Suites (PhotoShop and Illustrator); Microsoft Publisher, Preview, Microsoft Word and others. Simply open the software first and import document.

To use BITMAP (.bmp) images, you will require software that will allow you to view BITMAP images. You may use Adobe Acrobat Reader. For the latest free version, please visit http://www.adobe.com. You may also bring BITMAP images into a number of other image programs and design programs.

To use PDF images, you may use Adobe Acrobat Reader. For the latest free version, please visit http://www.adobe.com. You may also bring PDF images into a number of other image programs and design programs.

If image is larger than the page size of your printer, you will need to "tile" the image to print on multiple pages, and then assemble. Please consult your printer's user manual for tiling instructions. Or you may wish to visit your local office supply store, where larger format printers are available.

Most of the cross-stitch charts can simply be printed on standard printer paper. For piecing templates and embroidery templates, print at full size. Use a ruler to check the measurements as listed in the book.

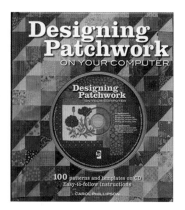

Designing Patchwork On Your Computer
by Carol Phillipson

Perfect for both beginners and more advanced stitchers, this book and CD offer step-by-step instruction on designing beautiful, eyecatching patchwork blocks using your computer. Why waste time and effort drawing and redrawing your designs by hand when you can try out as many designs as you like with just a few keystrokes? The book shows you how to design a wide range of patchwork blocks, and how to build your completed blocks into customized quilts and wall-hangings. The CD contains 100 ready-made templates, grids, and patchwork patterns to inspire your creativity.

Hardcover with CD-ROM; 8.25" × 9.25"; 128 pages; #Z0755
ISBN 13: 978-0-89689-400-6; ISBN 10: 0-89689-400-2

The Embroidery Stitch Bible
by Betty Barnden

More than 200 stitches are photographed and accompanied by easy-to-follow charts in this essential reference for embroiderers. From basic cross-stitch and chain stitch to more complicated couching, laid work, and drawn thread work, this is the stitch bible for embroiderers wishing to improve their technique and add new dimensions to their work. Stitches are arranged according to their use, including outlines, filling stitches, isolated stitches, motifs, edgings, hems, insertions, flat stitches, backgrounds and textures. Concealed spiral binding allows you to read and practice simultaneously.

Hardcover with concealed wire-o; 8" × 8"; 256 pages; #ESB
ISBN 13: 978-0-87349-510-3; ISBN 10: 0-87349-510-1

The Farmer's Wife Sampler Quilt
by Laurie Aaron Hird

In 1922, the very popular The Farmer's Wife magazine held a contest asking a simple question: "Would you want your daughter to marry a farmer?" Author Laurie Hird has excerpted 55 of the top letters and, using these letters as inspiration, she created 111 traditional 6" quilt blocks and created a tribute quilt. Each block is fully illustrated and comes with complete cutting templates on the bonus CD. In addition, she provides complete quiltmaking instructions for the queen-sized sampler quilt with all 111 blocks, as well as instruction on converting the quilt to lap, twin, double and king sizes.

Paperback with CD-ROM; 8" × 8"; 256 pages; #Z2991
ISBN 13: 978-0-89689-828-8; ISBN 10: 0-89689-828-8

These and other fine Krause Publications titles are available at your local craft retailer, bookstore or online supplier, or visit our website at www.mycraftivitystore.com.